asplashandadash!

COOKING WITH KEITH FLOYD

asplashandadash!

COOKING WITH **KEITH FLOYD**

Photography by Gareth Sambidge

CASSELL ILLUSTRATED

First published in Great Britain in 2006 by Cassell Illustrated,
a division of Octopus Publishing Group Limited
2-4 Heron Quays, London E14 4JP

A CIP catalogue record for this book is available from
the British Library.

ISBN-13: 978-1-844034-46-8
ISBN-10: 1-844034-46-1

10 9 8 7 6 5 4 3 2 1

Edited by Barbara Dixon and Robin Douglas-Withers
Designed by John Round Design
Food styling by Sunil Vijayakar

Keith Floyd is represented by Stan Green Management,
Dartmouth, Devon; telephone 01803 770046; fax 01803
770075; email tv@stangreen.co.uk; visit www.keithfloyd.co.uk

Printed in China

Recipe notes

Cups = teacup

Always sea salt and freshly ground black pepper unless
otherwise stated.

Eggs are medium unless otherwise stated.

Milk is full-fat milk.

Serving sizes = unless stated otherwise, all recipes will
feed approximately four people, depending on how
hungry you are and what you serve alongside it, in
keeping with the spirit of this book.

Contents

Introduction

During the Somerset winters of my boyhood in the mid 1950s, for me the best day of the week was Wednesday. At Wellington School we played rugby on Wednesday afternoons and, indeed, on Saturdays. But Wednesday was particularly special because when I, probably black-eyed, bloodied and bruised, cycled back to Wivelliscombe, I knew that supper would be faggots and peas dished up in a rich, thick gravy. My mother, Wynn, was an amazing cook and except when she was baking her bread (which she continued to do until the age of 85), or preparing her Christmas puddings and Christmas cakes in the early autumn, she never weighed, measured, calculated, timed or bothered much about oven temperatures at all. She was an inspirational cook, but moulded by financial circumstances that were not plentiful, and therefore the cottage garden and a degree of hunter-gathering were essential to her culinary plans.

She would prepare tripe and onions in a milky white sauce. She would get a ham hock and poach it in water flavoured with a bay leaf, thyme, parsley stalks and a carrot lifted from the garden. She would make a parsley sauce and soak butterbeans overnight and cook them gently until their skins cracked and revealed the soft texture of this wonderful pulse.

The day after she had cooked the ham and parsley sauce, she would have saved the liquor, bones and skin and prepared a green pea and ham stock soup, again with dried peas, or sometimes lentils, soaked overnight.

On other occasions she would buy an oxtail and simmer this with carrots and onions for hours until the glutinous flesh fell off the bone.

My mother did not know she was a good cook and much later in life I learned that she was ashamed of preparing these inexpensive, simple meals. She was never one to grill a steak, she couldn't have afforded it, but her liver and bacon with onion gravy was exceptional and I, as a very energetic boy, happily devoured everything she prepared.

In those halcyon days, after Sunday school, we would go on a family walk and pick peppery, crisp watercress from the local stream to make sandwiches for our afternoon tea. In the soft September mornings my sister Brenda and I were dispatched into the fields to gather horse mushrooms – wild, flat mushrooms that my mother first poached in milk and then fried in bacon fat.

During the summers we would collect, pricking our fingers, baskets of blackberries so that she could make her jam and her jelly, and when the elderberries came in we would pick those so that my father could make his curious elderberry wine.

Then, as autumn turned into winter, we would throw sticks into the chestnut trees and roll open the spiky shells with our feet, then take them home to be roasted in the fireplace, sucked out, squeezed out and flavoured with delicious salt.

We had no fridge, we had no convenience food, but there was a larder with a marble shelf where mother kept her pickled onions, her pickled eggs, her chutneys, jams and always a great wedge of Cheddar cheese wrapped in cheesecloth, and occasionally a chipped enamel bowl filled with clotted cream.

My father kept a few chickens in the garden, so we had a regular supply of fresh eggs and, from time to time, a beautifully roasted chicken served with giblet gravy and bread sauce.

Though none of these dishes appear in this book, it was my father's love of gardening and my mother's love of cooking that inspired me, fifty years ago, to become a cook. I would like to dedicate this book and its simple dishes to the memory of my parents.

in the soup

I don't see soups as a starter (a word I detest, by the way) as part of a three- or four-course meal, in an intimate and, invariably, stressful dinner party. In fact, I don't do dinner parties; I prefer to entertain at lunchtime.

Soups, by and large, are inexpensive and easy to make and many of them can be prepared well in advance and can then be frozen. I like to have soup as a dish in its own right, then a huge terrine, some wonderful fresh bread and a selection of red, white and rosé wines, followed by a platter of good cheeses, some good coffee and a large brandy.

You have all the time in the world to make a soup – you can do it today for tomorrow and reheat as required, either for lunch or supper. They are stress-free, satisfying and everyone loves them.

goulash soup

This fabulous soup, spicy and piquant, could almost be a lightweight stew. I recommend using shin of beef and, if possible, get hold of a nice marrowbone and remove it at the end of the cooking process. This will enrich the soup and give it a unique flavour.

Vegetable oil for frying

Onion 1 large, peeled and finely chopped

Stewing beef 225 g/8 oz, such as shin, skirt or chuck, cut into small cubes

Paprika 1 teaspoon

Caraway seeds a pinch of, crushed in a pestle and mortar

Beef stock 600 ml/1 pint

Garlic 1 clove, peeled and finely chopped

Green pepper ½, deseeded and cut into strips

Chopped tomatoes 400 g/13 oz can

Potatoes 2 medium, peeled and cubed

Salt and pepper

Heat a good splash of oil in a large heavy-based saucepan and sauté the onion until it is soft but not browned.

Add the meat and brown it lightly on all sides.

Sprinkle in a large pinch of salt, the paprika and caraway seeds and stir together, then add half the stock and mix thoroughly.

Add the garlic, green pepper and tomatoes and bring to the boil. Cover the pan with a lid, lower the heat to a gentle simmer and cook for about 1 hour, adding more stock if necessary to cover the meat.

Add the potato cubes with another pinch of salt and the remains of the stock and simmer until the potatoes are cooked – about another 30 minutes. Taste and season with salt and pepper.

Remove the soup from the heat and allow to cool, then skim off any fat.

Reheat and serve.

white onion soup

This is a classic, creamy, British soup and should be served hot. You can always top it with some small, butter-fried croutons and replace the parsley with chopped fresh chives or chervil. Yummy!

Unsalted butter 50 g/2 oz

Spanish onions 4 large, peeled and finely chopped

Celery sticks 2, stringed and finely chopped

Plain flour 50 g/2 oz

Milk 300 ml/10 fl oz

Chicken stock 900 ml/1½ pints good and hot

Nutmeg a pinch of freshly grated

Salt and pepper

To garnish

Single cream 150 ml/5 fl oz

Parsley a handful of fresh, finely chopped

Heat a little of the butter with 1 tablespoon of water in a pan and add the onions and celery. Cover the pan and sweat off the vegetables until they are nice and soft.

Tip the contents of the pan into a food processor or liquidizer and purée, then put to one side.

In the same pan, melt the remaining butter, add the flour and cook, stirring, over a medium heat until you have a creamy paste, otherwise known as a roux.

Add the milk, a dash at a time, whisking until you have a smooth, thick sauce.

Add the onion and celery purée and the hot stock and continue to heat and stir until you have a smooth soup.

Season with the nutmeg and salt and pepper to taste.

Serve in bowls with a swirl of cream and a scattering of chopped parsley on top.

orange and beetroot soup

This is a tangy, refreshing, summer soup. The sweetness of the beetroot and orange is balanced by the sherry. It has a spectacular, rich red colour, which can be enhanced by adding a swirl of cream or crème fraîche just before serving, and can be eaten either hot or cold.

Unsalted butter a large knob of

Spanish onions 2, peeled and roughly chopped

Beetroot 750 g/1½ lb cooked, peeled, roughly chopped

Potatoes 2 medium, peeled and roughly chopped

Vegetable stock 1.2 litres/2 pints

Dry or medium sherry 300 ml/10 fl oz

Orange juice 300 ml/10 fl oz

Salt and pepper

Orange zest to garnish

Serves 6

Heat the butter in a large heavy-based saucepan. Add the onions and fry over a medium heat, stirring until softened and turning golden.

Add the beetroot and potatoes and stir, then add the stock, sherry and orange juice. Bring to the boil, cover the pan and lower the heat. Simmer gently for 30–40 minutes. Take off the heat and leave to stand for about 10 minutes.

Tip the soup into a blender (do this in a couple of batches to save splattering) and whiz until smooth. Return to the saucepan, season with salt and pepper and reheat gently.

Serve garnished with orange zest.

summer vegetable soup with basil

This recipe is great for crowds of friends. Don't overcook the vermicelli.

Olive oil for frying

Garlic 5 cloves, peeled and finely chopped

Tomatoes 750 g/1½ lb, peeled, deseeded and chopped

Water 2 litres/3½ pints

White haricot beans 450 g/1 lb canned, drained and rinsed

Kidney beans 450 g/1 lb canned, drained and rinsed

Potatoes 3, peeled and cubed

Courgettes 450 g/1 lb, peeled and cubed

Green beans 450 g/1 lb, trimmed and cut into 2.5 cm/1 inch lengths

Broad beans 450 g/1 lb fresh, shelled

Basil leaves 2 handfuls of fresh, chopped

Vermicelli 2 handfuls

Salt and pepper

Parmesan cheese a large handful of freshly grated, to serve

Heat a large splash of olive oil in a very large pan, add half the garlic and fry gently for 30 seconds or so, then add the tomatoes, water and a dash of salt. Bring to the boil, add the drained beans, lower the heat and simmer for 15 minutes.

Add the potatoes, courgettes, green beans and broad beans, cover the pan and simmer for 25–30 minutes.

While the soup is simmering, mash the remaining garlic and the basil to a thick paste in a pestle and mortar (or you can use a food processor). Stir this paste into the soup, add the vermicelli and cook gently for a further 5 minutes.

Season and serve sprinkled with the grated Parmesan.

brown onion soup

This legendary soup was made famous in the markets of Paris. The porters, the fishmongers, the butchers *et al*, having started work very early, would eat it for breakfast, while dishevelled dinner-jacketed men and elegantly dressed women would stumble in from a night on the tiles and take it as a hangover cure.

Unsalted butter 75 g/3 oz

Spanish onions 750 g/1½ lb, peeled, halved and finely sliced

Garlic 3 cloves, peeled and very finely chopped

Plain flour 1 tablespoon

Red wine 200 ml/7 fl oz

Beef stock 1.5 litres/2½ pints

bouquet garni (fresh thyme, parsley stalks and 1 bay leaf, tied together with string)

French bread 1 stick

Gruyère cheese 75 g/3 oz, grated

Salt and pepper

Serves 6

Heat the butter in a large heavy-based saucepan. Add the onions and cook very slowly, stirring all the time, over a fairly low heat to soften the onions and brown them gently – about 30 minutes.

Stir in the garlic, then add the flour, stirring well to mix everything with no lumps, and cook for about 1 minute.

Pour in the wine and allow the mixture to bubble until the wine has reduced a little.

Add the stock and mix well, then add the bouquet garni and season with salt and pepper.

Bring the soup back to the boil, then lower the heat, cover the pan and simmer gently for about 30 minutes.

Remove the bouquet garni and discard, then leave the soup to cool a little.

Meanwhile, cut the French stick into thick slices and toast on both sides.

Pour a third of the soup into a blender and blend until smooth, then tip back into the pan and reheat, stirring well. Season with salt and pepper as necessary.

Preheat the grill to very hot. Pour the soup into serving bowls, float a couple of pieces of toasted bread onto each of the bowls, sprinkle liberally with the Gruyère cheese and pop under the hot grill until the cheese has melted and is golden brown. Serve immediately.

creamy smoked fish soup

A rich, rib-sticking, tummy-pleasing chowder. A wonderful winter's day lunch dish. Please bear in mind that if you do not want to use haddock, some smoked cod or another white fish will be a perfectly good substitute. However, you cannot use an oily fish such as mackerel or herring as it will not work.

Milk 1.2 litres/2 pints

Celery sticks 2, stringed and finely chopped

Spanish onions 2, peeled and finely chopped

Bay leaves 2

Fresh parsley 1 large sprig

White peppercorns 6

Smoked haddock fillets 450 g/1 lb skinless and boneless

Unsalted butter 50 g/2 oz

Garlic 1 clove, peeled and very finely chopped

Dry sherry 150 ml/5 fl oz

Smoked ham 125 g/4 oz piece, diced

Potato 1 large, peeled and finely diced

Sweetcorn 198 g/7 oz can, drained

Smoked salmon 150 g/5 oz, chopped

Double cream 2 tablespoons

Parsley a good handful of chopped fresh, to garnish

Heat the milk in a shallow pan, add the celery, half the onions, the bay leaves, parsley sprig and peppercorns. Add the smoked haddock, bring to a simmer and poach for 1 minute. Remove from the heat and set aside to cool.

Remove the fish from the poaching liquid and flake, then set aside. Strain the poaching liquid into a bowl and set aside.

Melt the butter in a large saucepan, add the rest of the onions and the garlic and fry gently for a few minutes until soft but not browned.

Pour in the sherry, increase the heat and boil until it has almost entirely evaporated.

Add the ham, potato and sweetcorn and stir in the poaching liquid. Bring this mixture up to a simmer and simmer gently for about 20 minutes.

Stir in the haddock flakes and the smoked salmon, pour in the cream and heat gently.

Serve sprinkled with the chopped parsley.

watercress soup

One of my favourites – quick to make but quite delicious! It has a lovely peppery flavour and is creamy, too. The finished soup should be a vibrant green colour. You can serve it either hot or cold.

Watercress 2 thick bunches of fresh

Unsalted butter 50 g/2 oz

Spanish onion 1, peeled and finely chopped

Plain flour 2 tablespoons

Milk 600 ml/1 pint

Vegetable or chicken stock 300 ml/10 fl oz

Single cream 150 ml/5 fl oz

Nutmeg freshly grated

Salt and pepper

Prepare the watercress by discarding any woody stalks, then chop roughly.

Melt the butter in a large saucepan, add the onion and fry gently over a medium heat until softened but not brown.

Sprinkle in the flour and cook gently, stirring all the time, until well amalgamated.

Slowly add the milk, whisking all the time, then add the stock. Keep whisking until smooth and thickened. Season to taste with salt and pepper.

Allow to cool a little, then add the watercress and immediately pour into a blender or food processor and whiz until smooth.

Pour into a saucepan, add the cream and heat through.

Grate over a little nutmeg just before serving. This soup can be served hot or chilled.

chicken soup with egg and lemon

A highly digestible broth with a citrus tang. I recommend using a boiling fowl for this soup as it will have more flavour – ask your butcher. If you can't obtain one, use a normal chicken. Once it has been simmered, it will be good for nothing, but your cat might enjoy it!

Chicken 1 medium

Spanish onion 1 large, peeled

Rice 1 cup

Plain flour 1 tablespoon

Lemon juice of 1

Eggs 2

Salt and pepper

Put the chicken in a very large pan and cover with water. Bring to the boil, then lower the heat and skim off any foam or scum. Add the onion and season with salt and pepper, then cover the pan and simmer for 1–1¼ hours.

Remove the chicken and the onion from the broth and discard. Add the rice to the broth and simmer for about another 15 minutes until the rice is cooked. Set aside 1 cup of broth to cool.

To prepare the egg and lemon mixture, mix the flour with the lemon juice in a bowl until smooth. Beat the eggs into the flour and lemon juice, then add the cup of cooled soup broth and mix well.

Serve the chicken broth in bowls and pour over the lemon sauce.

beer soup

This literally is a splash and a dash! It may seem strange to use beer, but that beer and stout are not unusual ingredients in stews and so forth. It has a uniquely yeasty flavour and we all have some beer in the fridge.

Unsalted butter a knob of

Onion 1, peeled and finely chopped

Chicken stock 1 litre/1¾ pints

Strong lager 750 ml/1¼ pints

Fine white breadcrumbs 50 g/2 oz

Double cream 150 ml/5 fl oz

Nutmeg freshly grated

Salt and pepper

slices of bread, cut into squares and fried in oil for the croûton garnish

Serves 4–6

Heat the butter in a pan, add the onion and cook gently until softened.

Add the stock and lager and bring to the boil.

Stir in the breadcrumbs until they are completely absorbed and the soup has thickened.

Stir in the cream and season with nutmeg, salt and pepper to taste.

Serve garnished with the croûtons.

sherried fish
soup

This is a hearty and unusual soup. Keep the fish in good-sized chunks, and be careful not to overcook it. You could always add some very finely crushed garlic to the mayonnaise and have a very chilled bottle of Manzanilla sherry to sip with it.

Water or fish stock 1.5 litres/2½ pints

White fish fillets 500 g/1 lb 2 oz, such as hake, haddock, cod, etc.

Raw prawns 250 g/9 oz peeled, fresh, deveined if large

Frozen peas 100 g/3½ oz

Cooked ham 40 g/1½ oz, chopped

Pimiento 1 canned, chopped

Mayonnaise 225 ml/8 fl oz

Lemon juice 1 tablespoon

Dry sherry 50 ml/2 fl oz

Salt and pepper

Lemon wedges, to garnish

Serves 6

Pour the water or stock into a large saucepan and bring to a simmer.

Add the fish fillets and cook for 5 minutes, then add the prawns and cook until they just turn pink.

Strain the soup, put aside the fish and prawns and return the soup stock to the pan.

When cool enough to handle, flake the fish and remove any remaining skin and bones.

Add the peas, ham and pimiento to the soup stock and continue to simmer until the peas are tender.

Beat the mayonnaise in a bowl with the lemon juice until smooth and creamy, then beat in the sherry.

Return the fish and prawns to the soup mixture and season to taste, then keep at a low simmer.

Pour one ladleful of the soup onto the mayonnaise mixture, beating constantly, then pour the mayonnaise mixture into the soup. Do not boil.

Serve garnished with lemon wedges.

oxtail soup

I must confess this soup does take some time to cook and is best left overnight in the fridge so that you can remove the fat that will have floated to the surface before you shred the meat from the bones. It will have been worth it.

Unsalted butter 50 g/2 oz

Oxtail pieces 450 g/1 lb

Plain flour 2 tablespoons seasoned

Spanish onions 2 medium, peeled and finely chopped

Celery sticks 2, stringed and finely chopped

Lean ham or bacon 50 g/2 oz, cubed

Beef stock 900 ml/1½ pints

Red wine 1 wine glass

Bay leaf 1

Cloves 2

Carrot 1 medium

Worcestershire sauce or bottled anchovy sauce a dash of

Cornflour 1 dessertspoon

Sherry 1 small glass

Olive oil for frying

Salt and pepper

Heat the butter and a splash of oil in a large heavy-based pan.

Dust the oxtail in the seasoned flour and cook in the pan until browned on all sides.

Add the onions, celery and ham or bacon and fry until golden.

Pour in the stock and wine, add the bay leaf and cloves and grind in some black pepper. Bring to the boil, then lower the heat, cover the pan and simmer very, very gently for 4–5 hours. Check occasionally to make sure it is not drying out.

Strain off the liquid and leave to get cold. You can leave this overnight. When completely cold, the fat will have solidified on the top of the stock. Remove the fat completely.

Remove all the meat from the oxtail and discard the bones. Cut the meat into small pieces and set aside. Peel and grate the carrot.

Put the strained, skimmed soup stock into a pan, add the grated carrot and Worcestershire or anchovy sauce, cover the pan and simmer for about 40 minutes.

Mix the cornflour with the sherry until smooth, then add to the soup, bring to the boil and stir until thickened.

Add the oxtail meat to the soup to reheat, season with salt and pepper and serve hot.

pea and macaroni soup

Unless you are lucky enough to grow your own peas, you really cannot beat good-quality frozen petit pois, which, by the way, you cook from frozen. In my opinion, frozen peas are sweeter and definitely add more flavour.

Olive oil for frying

Onion 1, peeled and finely chopped

Petit pois 1 kg/2¼ lb frozen

Chicken or vegetable stock 1 litre/1¾ pints

Small macaroni 200 g/7 oz cooked

Parmesan cheese a handful of freshly grated

Salt and pepper

Serves 6

Heat a good splash of oil in a large heavy-based saucepan and sauté the onion until softened.

Add the peas, then pour in the stock and bring to a simmer. Cook for 10–15 minutes, or until the peas begin to disintegrate.

Season with salt and pepper and add the cooked macaroni.

Sprinkle generously with the grated Parmesan and serve.

flash in
a pan

Stir-frying, poaching and frying are all quick methods of cooking that can be done on top of the stove. They also enable you to show off your flair and expertise. It is a very creative way of cooking since you can add things as you go along as you wish. You can also use alcohol, since flambéeing will quickly burn off the alcohol and leave just the flavour of the wine or spirit.

As usual, careful shopping, planning and preparation are paramount. It is essential, when cooking meat, to buy the most tender cuts and, in some cases, to cut the meat into strips to cook quickly. Many people come to grief with the cookery book in one hand while trying to peel onions with the other. Have all your prepared peeled or chopped ingredients neatly arranged on plastic trays or in bowls or plastic boxes. If you are following a recipe, read it carefully and be prepared to apply a little latitude and commonsense.

tartare of salmon
or sea trout or
char with a
celeriac rösti

Salmon is a richer fish than sea trout, which is really a combination of trout and salmon. Both are farmed nowadays, although they are best wild. Celeriac is a delicate vegetable and will not overwhelm the flavour of the fish.

Salmon, sea trout, trout or char 1, about 900 g/2 lb, skinned, filleted and any bones removed

Caviar (salmon, sturgeon or lumpfish) 125 g/4 oz

Crème fraîche 4 tablespoons

Fresh dill or parsley, to garnish

For the marinade

Fresh root ginger 2.5 cm/1 inch piece of, peeled and grated

Red chilli 1, deseeded and finely chopped

Limes zest and juice of 2

Groundnut or light oil 150 ml/5 fl oz

Salt a pinch

Caster sugar a pinch

For the rösti

Celeriac 2 bulbs of, peeled and cut into quarters

White onion 1 large, peeled and quartered

Clarified butter 125 g/4 oz

Salt and pepper

Chill the fish fillets in the freezer for at least 30 minutes.

Mix all the ingredients for the marinade.

Remove the fish from the freezer and slice very thinly into strips. Place the fish in a shallow dish and pour over the marinade, making sure all the fish is well coated. Put to one side while you make the rösti.

For the rösti, grate the celeriac and onion and pat dry with kitchen paper to remove excess moisture.

Melt 2 tablespoons of the clarified butter and mix with the onion and celeriac, season well with salt and pepper and form into four small patties about 5 cm/2 inches round and 1 cm/½ inch thick.

Heat the remaining clarified butter in a pan and fry the patties until golden and crisp on both sides.

To serve, place a rösti on each plate and arrange a few slices of the marinated fish fillet over it. Spoon on some crème fraîche and top with caviar, then drizzle with a little of the marinade and garnish with dill or parsley.

herring fillets with lemon and mustard cream

As much as creamy horseradish titillates roast beef, so does a mustard sauce enhance a herring – it is your choice whether you use smooth or grain mustard. I would recommend grain.

Herring fillets 8

Plain flour 50 g/2 oz seasoned

Unsalted butter 50 g/2 oz

Lemons juice of 2

Dijon mustard 2 teaspoons

Double cream 150 ml/5 fl oz

Egg yolks 2

Salt and pepper

Fresh dill or chopped chives, to garnish

Dust the herring fillets with the flour, then pat off any excess.

Melt three-quarters of the butter in a heavy-based frying pan and fry the herring fillets for a couple of minutes on each side. Remove from the pan and place on a dish to keep warm. Retain the juices in the pan.

Add the lemon juice to the hot pan and stir to deglaze the pan juices. Whisk in the mustard and 1 tablespoon of the cream until smooth.

Lower the heat, add the remaining butter and cream and the egg yolks and whisk until smooth and thickened. Season to taste.

Arrange the herrings on a warm dish and, using a sieve, pour over the sauce. Garnish with dill or chives and serve.

potato waffle, salmon eggs and soured cream

This light luncheon can be enjoyed with seriously frozen vodka or aquavit since it is, in reality, a Scandinavian dish.

For the potato waffle

Self-raising flour 250 g/9 oz

Eggs 2

Single cream 125 ml/4 fl oz

Milk 300 ml/10 fl oz

Unsalted butter 125 g/4 oz melted, cooled

Potato 175 g/6 oz, peeled and grated

Vegetable oil for frying

Salt and white pepper

For the garnish

Rocket leaves a handful of

Olive oil 2 tablespoons

Lemon juice of ½

Soured cream 300 ml/10 fl oz thick

Black lumpfish roe 175 g/6 oz

Red lumpfish roe 175 g/6 oz

Red salmon roe 175 g/6 oz

Red onion 1, peeled and finely chopped

Quails' eggs 4, hard-boiled and halved

To make the waffle mixture, sieve the flour into a large bowl. In a jug, whisk together the eggs, cream, milk and melted butter until well mixed. Make a well in the centre of the flour and pour in the wet ingredients, whisking well with the flour until you have a smooth batter. Beat in the grated potato and season with salt and pepper. Cover and set aside in the fridge to rest for a couple of hours.

Using either a waffle iron or a very heavy-based frying pan, heat a splash of vegetable oil and pour in the waffle batter. Fry the batter until golden on both sides and slightly puffed up.

Place on a plate and divide the waffle into 4 wedges.

To serve, place a handful of rocket leaves on a serving dish and sprinkle over the olive oil and lemon juice. Top each waffle wedge with soured cream and spoon on the caviars, then sprinkle over some chopped onion and top with 2 egg halves.

shellfish in champagne sauce

Cooking with champagne will give a lighter result than white wine. First chill your magnum of dry champagne or Spanish cava and then use another bottle to make the sauce!

Unsalted butter and olive oil for frying

Garlic 4 cloves, peeled and finely chopped

Shallots 5, peeled and finely chopped

Mediterranean prawns, Dublin bay prawns or freshwater crayfish 2 kg/4½ lb peeled, raw (defrosted if frozen)

Marc de champagne 1 glass (strong spirit made from the residue of champagne grape pressings)

Fish stock 270 ml/9 fl oz

Brut champagne 1 bottle

Double cream 300 ml/10 fl oz

Black truffles 2, finely sliced

Saffron strands a pinch of

Salt and pepper

Fresh parsley a good handful of, finely chopped, to garnish

Serves 6–8

Heat a large knob of butter and a good splash of oil in a large sauté pan, add the garlic and shallots and cook until soft.

Add the shellfish, stirring them in the pan until they are turning pink, then add the marc and set alight. When the flames have subsided, add the fish stock and champagne and bring to the boil, then reduce the heat and simmer for 2–3 minutes until the shellfish are completely red. Remove the shellfish from the pan and set aside to keep warm.

To finish the sauce, briskly boil the cooking liquid until reduced by half.

Lower the heat and whisk in the cream, truffles and saffron and season with salt and pepper. Whisk in a knob of butter to produce a smooth sauce.

Return the shellfish to the sauce and warm through, then pile on to a serving dish and sprinkle over the chopped parsley.

mussels with orange and saffron

The best mussels come from the cold waters that surround the British Isles. I once had a friend who served so many mussels, he cleaned them in his wife's washing machine in a cold water rinse. But just remember to scrape off any barnacles, take off the beard and make sure they are free of sand.

Mussels 1.4 kg/3 lb, cleaned, beards removed and well rinsed

Dry white wine 1 wine glass

Fish stock 600 ml/1 pint

Shallot 1, peeled and finely chopped

Double cream 125 ml/4 fl oz

Saffron a pinch of

Orange grated zest and juice of 1

Leek 1, cut into thin strips 2.5 cm/1 inch long

Carrot 1, peeled and cut into thin strips 2.5 cm/1 inch long

Celery 1 stick, stringed and cut into thin strips 2.5 cm/1 inch long

Salt and pepper

Discard any mussels that are open and will not close when given a sharp tap. Put the mussels, wine, stock and shallot into a large pan, cover with a tight-fitting lid and steam over a high heat, shaking the pan occasionally, until the mussels have opened – 3–4 minutes.

Strain the mussels, reserving the cooking liquid. Discard any mussels that have not opened. Remove the mussels from their shells and put to one side. To remove any grit, strain the cooking liquid through a fine sieve into a pan and boil until it has reduced by half.

Add the cream, saffron, orange zest and juice and vegetable strips to the mussel liquid and bring to the boil. Add the mussels, season and serve immediately.

gratin of mussels or clams

If you are using young spinach, strip the leaves from the stalks and discard the stalks; if, however, you like the idea of Swiss chard, which is a wonderful alternative, blanch the chopped stalks and boil in salted water, then lightly boil the shredded leaves.

Fresh mussels 1.4–1.75 kg/3–4 lb, cleaned and beards removed, or fresh large clams, well rinsed

Dry white wine 1 large wine glass

Unsalted butter 25 g/1 oz

Plain flour 2 tablespoons

Milk a dash of

Double cream 150 ml/5 fl oz

Nutmeg a pinch of freshly grated

Fresh spinach 4 cups finely chopped, cooked

Parmesan cheese 3 tablespoons finely grated fresh

Pepper

Discard any mussels or clams that are open and will not close when given a sharp tap. Put the mussels or clams into a large pan, add the wine, cover with a tight-fitting lid and steam over a medium heat, shaking the pan occasionally, until the shells are all open – 3–4 minutes.

Strain the mussels or clams, reserving the cooking liquid. Discard any that have not opened. Remove any grit by straining the cooking liquid through a fine sieve.

Preheat the grill. Melt the butter in a pan, stir in the flour and cook until you have a smooth roux (paste). Add a dash of milk to the cooking liquor to make up about 150 ml/5 fl oz of liquid and slowly whisk into the roux over a medium heat to make a smooth sauce. Stir in the cream and season with the nutmeg and pepper.

Spread the cooked spinach over the bottom of an ovenproof gratin dish and sprinkle over the cooked mussels or clams. Pour the sauce over the top, sprinkle with the grated Parmesan and put under the grill until the cheese is hot and golden. Serve with a green salad.

scallops spiced with lime

Once again we see the harmonious marriage of citrus fruits, petit pois and top-quality shellfish. If you cannot get limes, you could use lemons, but I always prefer the taste of lime.

Dry white wine 2 wine glasses

Scallops 500 g/1 lb 2 oz, corals removed

Petit pois 1 cup cooked

For the lime dressing

Pastis or Pernod a dash of

Chilli sauce a dash of

Lime juice of 1

Good red wine vinegar 1 tablespoon

Olive oil 2 tablespoons

Salt and pepper

Place all the ingredients for the lime dressing in a small jar, replace the lid and shake well until all they are combined. Season with salt and pepper and set aside.

Pour the wine into a pan and bring to a simmer, then add the scallops and poach for about 3 minutes, or until just tender. Remove the scallops and set aside on a warm serving dish.

Add the lime dressing and petit pois to the cooking liquor and warm over a low heat.

Pour the sauce over the scallops and serve immediately.

cod with bacon and red pepper sauce

Cod is such a wonderful fish and red peppers are such a wonderful vegetable, this harmonious marriage of the two will delight you.

Red pepper 1 large, blanched whole, deseeded and skin removed

Double cream 150 ml/5 fl oz

Fish stock 300 ml/10 fl oz

Unsalted butter a large knob of

Cod fillets 6 fresh unskinned

Fine white breadcrumbs 75 g/3 oz

Smoked streaky bacon 225 g/8 oz piece of, rind removed and cut into lardons

Salt and pepper

Serves 6

Preheat the grill to hot. Liquidize the red pepper with the cream and strain through a fine sieve. Pour into a pan and heat gently, adding enough stock to make a thin sauce. Season with salt and pepper and keep it warm.

Next, heat the butter in a frying pan and fry the cod fillets skin-side only for a couple of minutes. Turn them over, sprinkle with the breadcrumbs, place a knob of butter on each fillet and place under the hot grill until the fish is cooked through and the breadcrumbs have formed a golden crust.

While the fish is grilling, fry the bacon lardons until they are golden and crunchy.

Pour the red pepper sauce onto a serving dish, place the fish on top and scatter the bacon over the lot.

coquilles saint-jacques au gratin

As I have said elsewhere in this book, scallops are one of my favourite molluscs and this old-fashioned way of preparing them is just a joy.

Scallops 4 large, white meat only (not the coral)

Shallots 2, peeled and finely chopped

Chanterelle mushrooms 250 g/9 oz, finely chopped

Dry white wine 1 small glass

Plain flour 1 tablespoon

Double cream 150 ml/5 fl oz

Parmesan cheese 1 tablespoon finely grated

Unsalted butter a large knob of

Salt and pepper

Preheat the grill to hot. Slice the scallops into fine discs.

Heat a little butter in a pan and gently sauté the shallots until they are soft but not coloured. Add the mushrooms and continue to cook until the mushrooms are softened.

Add the wine to the pan and bring to a simmer. Drop in the scallops and poach for about 30 seconds, then remove and set aside.

In another pan, melt the butter over a medium heat, add the flour and cook, stirring, until you have a smooth roux (paste). Cook for a couple of minutes, then add the shallots, mushrooms and cooking liquor and whisk well to make a sauce. Add the cream to enrich the sauce, then season with salt and pepper.

Arrange the scallops in small dishes or scallop shells and pour over the sauce. Sprinkle over the grated Parmesan and pop under the hot grill until bubbling and golden. Serve at once.

poached fish
fillets with
green pea sauce

This is not exactly deep-fried haddock in batter with mushy peas, but little green peas do make a superb sauce for delicate fillets of fish.

Fish stock 600 ml/1 pint

Pastis or Pernod a good dash of

Fresh horseradish 2–3 teaspoons, grated, plus extra to garnish

Halibut or similar firm white fish 4 fillets of, each about 175 g/6 oz, skinned

For the green pea sauce

Frozen peas 175 g/6 oz

Unsalted butter 25 g/1 oz

Double cream 2 tablespoons

Fresh mint 1 tablespoon chopped

Salt and pepper

For the vegetable garnish

Celery sticks 2, stringed and cut into fine batons about 5 cm/2 inches in length

Carrots 2, peeled and cut into batons as above

Spring onions 6, trimmed and cut into strips

Green beans a handful of fine,

Asparagus spears a bunch of fine

Fresh mint leaves a handful of

To prepare the vegetable garnish, place all the vegetables into a steamer, sprinkle over the mint leaves and steam for 8–10 minutes, or until the vegetables are cooked but still firm.

For the sauce, put the peas in a saucepan, just cover with water and simmer for 5–6 minutes until they are just cooked. Drain and place in a food processor with the butter and whiz to a purée. Return to the saucepan and heat gently.

Meanwhile, heat the stock, pastis or Pernod and the horseradish in a frying pan or shallow sauté pan. Add the fish fillets and simmer for about 5 minutes, or until the fish is opaque and cooked. Gently remove the fillets and set aside in a warm place.

To finish off the sauce, add 1 tablespoon of the fish liquor to the pea purée, add the cream and mint and heat gently, stirring all the time until you have a smooth sauce. Taste and season.

Pour the sauce onto a serving dish, arrange the fish and steamed vegetables on top and grate over a little extra horseradish as a garnish.

Stir-fried pork or chicken

If you have a halogen hob – forget this dish. Take out the calor gas camping stove and cook it outside. It needs fierce heat.

Buy some **fillet of pork** or **breast of chicken**, as much as you want or as much as you need. Buy a **red pepper** and a **green pepper**, some really vibrant **spring onions**, some **fresh root ginger**, a **fresh pineapple**, some **very hot chillies**, a big bunch of **fresh coriander**, some **Thai fish sauce** and **soy sauce**.

Slice the meat thinly. Remove the pith and seeds from the peppers and cut into fine strips. Cut the spring onions into finger-length pieces, then peel the ginger and cut into very fine slices. Oh, I forgot to tell you, have some **garlic** as well, peeled and finely chopped. Cut the pineapple into small cubes (peel it first, of course), then chop the chillies and the coriander.

Now, heat some vegetable oil in a pan, stir-fry the meat and peppers until the meat has taken on some colour, then add the chillies and garlic, then the pineapple, spring onions and ginger. Add a dash of fish sauce and a dash of soy sauce. Cook very quickly and garnish with the coriander just before serving.

P.S. If you want to, you can throw in some **cherry tomatoes** cut in half.

quick stir-fried
chicken curry

Use fresh chicken for this dish. Leftover cooked chicken will never have the right texture. Cut the chicken into small strips and it will cook very quickly. Spiciness is the nicyness of lifyness!

First prepare your spicy ingredients, which are as follows: about a tablespoon of **coriander seeds**, the same of **ground turmeric**, half the amount of **cumin seeds** and **cloves**, a **cinnamon stick**, two or three peeled **red shallots,** a handful of **fresh green chillies**, a handful of **fresh mint leaves**, a handful of **fresh coriander leaves**, a piece of peeled **fresh root ginger**, a few peeled **garlic cloves**, a pinch of **caster sugar**, **salt** and **white wine vinegar**.

Dry roast all the spices until they release their aroma, then throw them into a food processor with the shallots, chillies, herbs, ginger, garlic, sugar, a pinch of salt and enough of the vinegar to make a paste.

Now, fry some slices of **chicken breast** until just cooked. Stir in your lovely paste, cook out the paste for a couple of minutes and moisten with either a little **chicken stock** or some **coconut milk**.

Garnish with torn up **fresh basil leaves**.

spicy beef

Put some spice into your life. As with all recipes, adjust the chilli to your taste. The rule of thumb is that the seeds and pith are where the heat is, so you can remove them if you wish.

You will need a handful of **dried red chillies**, some **cumin seeds**, **black peppercorns**, **ground turmeric**, **cloves**, a **cinnamon stick**, a peeled **head of garlic**, a piece of peeled, **fresh root ginger**, some **caster sugar** and **red wine vinegar**. Have on hand some finely chopped **red onions** and **red peppers**, **coconut milk** and **fresh coriander**.

In a dry frying pan, dry roast all the spices (you need about 1 tablespoon of each of them, except the cinnamon stick) until they give off their aroma. Then throw them into a coffee grinder or small food processor with the garlic, ginger and a pinch of sugar and whiz with enough of the vinegar to make a paste (masala).

You will also need a **fillet of beef** (as much as you think you need); cut this into strips.

Now, heat a splash of **vegetable oil** in a hot pan and fry the red onions, strips of red pepper and the fillet of beef. Just before they are cooked, add in the masala and stir-fry for a few moments. Add a splash of coconut milk and continue to cook until the beef is tender.

Serve sprinkled with fresh coriander.

minced beef risotto

This is a very unusual risotto, rich and satisfyingly filling. Parmesan cheese goes incredibly well with beef and this is an excellent dish to serve for supper.

Beef stock about 600 ml/1 pint

Unsalted butter a big knob of

Red onions 2, peeled and finely chopped

Garlic 2 cloves, peeled and crushed

Minced beef 350 g/12 oz

Short grained rice 200 g/7 oz

Red pepper 1, deseeded, pith removed and finely diced

Dry white wine a good slosh of

Ground paprika a pinch of

Capers a handful of, rinsed and coarsely chopped

Lemon juice of ½

Salt and pepper

To serve

Parmesan cheese a handful of freshly grated

Fresh parsley chopped

The most important thing with any risotto is to keep the stock hot, so place it in a separate pan and keep on the heat.

Heat the butter in a large heavy-based pan and sauté the onions and garlic until they are softened and just turning golden. Add the mince and stir-fry over a medium heat, stirring with a spatula, until cooked and all the meat has separated.

Stir in the rice and mix well, then add the diced pepper. Slosh in the wine and stir again, then slowly add the hot stock, a ladle at a time. Keep stirring until the liquid has been absorbed before adding the next ladle. Repeat the process until all the stock is used up and the rice is tender.

Add the paprika and season with salt and pepper, then add the capers and lemon juice and stir in well. Serve sprinkled with the grated Parmesan and chopped parsley.

lamb hash

This is the perfect way to use your leftover roast lamb and it makes a great change from a shepherd's pie. You could substitute leftover roast beef for lamb in this dish, but not chicken or pork – they will not work.

Unsalted butter 2 large knobs of

Onion 1, peeled and chopped

Potato a large or two, peeled and cut into very small cubes

Leftover roast lamb, cut into cubes

Worcestershire sauce a dash of

Tabasco sauce a dash of

Eggs 2

Salt and pepper

Fresh parsley chopped, to garnish

Melt a large knob of butter in a heavy-based frying pan and add the onion. Cook until nicely browned, then remove from the pan with a slotted spoon and set aside.

Melt some more butter and add the potato. Cook, stirring occasionally, until browned and tender.

Add the lamb and continue to cook until the lamb has warmed through and coloured slightly, then tip the onions back in.

Mix everything well, then add a dash of Worcestershire and a dash of Tabasco sauce and season with salt and pepper. Place the hash on a serving dish and keep warm.

Fry the eggs in a little butter, then place them on top of the hash and garnish with chopped parsley.

lamb cutlets
with mint and
apple salsa

The tangy, refreshing taste of the mint and apple salsa will make tender young cutlets so delicious your guests will refuse to leave until they have had seconds.

Chop up a bunch of **fresh mint leaves** and some peeled and cored **eating apples** and put in a bowl. Add a tablespoon of **caster sugar**, some grated, peeled **fresh root ginger** and a dash of **white wine vinegar**. Mix all these ingredients and leave aside in the fridge for 4–5 hours.

Buy the best **lamb cutlets** that you can find and sear them in a dry pan with sprigs of **rosemary** until done to your liking. Remove the now burnt rosemary and anoint the cutlets with the exotic mint and apple salsa.

ham and lettuce lasagne

This is a superb summer supper or lunch dish. It has nothing to do with pasta and everything to do with style and taste. Always use firm lettuce.

First make a lovely cheese sauce. To do this, heat some **milk** with an **onion** and **cloves** to infuse. Melt some **unsalted butter** in a heavy-based saucepan, add some **plain flour** and stir to make a smooth roux (paste). Strain the milk, pour into the roux and continue to whisk well until you have a thick sauce. Grate in plenty of well-flavoured **cheese** – this can be your choice, add a teaspoon of **mustard**, a dash of **Worcestershire sauce** and season well with **salt** and **pepper**.

Take several slices of **cooked ham** and several **crunchy lettuces** such as Little Gems. Chop up the lettuce and layer it between the slices of ham in a heatproof dish. Pour over the sauce, grate some more cheese on the top and pop under a hot grill until bubbling and golden.

floyd's pork

I suppose you could call this an instant delight – it takes seconds to cook and is actually delicious. As with all delicate meats, do not overcook fillet of pork. Unlike other cuts, it does not have the fat content to protect it.

Cut some **fillet of pork** into very fine slices and season with **salt** and **pepper**. Peel and core half a dozen **eating apple**s and cut into small pieces.

Put a large knob of **unsalted butter** into a pan and fry the pork until just cooked. Add the apples, then pour in some **Calvados** and set alight. When the flames subside, stir in some **double cream**, season with a pinch of **ground cinnamon** and thicken the sauce with another knob of butter.

chicken livers with marsala

This is a very quick yet rich dish. It's also economical and satisfying, particularly if you serve it on a wonderful crispy fried slice of bread. As with all livers, if they are over-cooked they will become bitter.

Take a tub or two of **chicken livers**, trim and cut into largish chunks, then dust with **seasoned flour**. Heat up some **unsalted butter** in a heavy-based pan and fry the chicken livers on each side until golden but still pink in the middle.

Pour in a good splash of **marsala** and set alight. When the flames subside, stir well and add a dash of **double cream**, enough to just give you a sauce. Season with **salt** and **pepper** and serve garnished with **chopped parsley**.

calves' liver with onion sauce

This delicate liver is lightly seared and served a little pink to allow the juices to blend beautifully with the onion sauce. Always serve liver pink – if it is overcooked, it will become tough and grainy.

Peel a load of **white onions**, and slice them very, very finely, then sauté them in **butter** until they are soft.

Meanwhile, warm some **milk** (according to how many onions you have) with a **chopped carrot**, a piece of chopped **celery** and a **bay leaf**. When this has infused well, strain it into a jug.

Now, stir some **plain flour** into your softly sautéed onions, to make a bit of a roux, then strain the warmed, infused milk into that mixture. Stir well to remove any lumps, then stir until the sauce is rich and unctuous and season with **salt** and **pepper**. Now pour the sauce into a food processor and whiz until you have a delicious, creamy onion sauce.

Take some slices of **calves' liver** and pop them into a very hot pan, flipping them from side to side until they are cooked, but pink in the middle. Serve with the puréed onion sauce.

This is a sauce that Escoffier called *Sauce Soubise*.

lambs' liver stroganoff

These little goujons of lambs' liver, quickly tossed in butter or oil and mixed with the wonderful sauce, will delight even those who have an aversion to offal.

Soften some thinly sliced **onions** in **unsalted butter** over a gentle heat and put aside. Sauté some finely sliced **button mushrooms** in the same butter, then put them to one side.

Slice some **lambs' liver** into thin strips and roll them in **flour** seasoned with **paprika**.

Heat some more butter in a heavy-based frying pan and quickly sear the lambs' liver on both sides. Add the cooked onions and mushrooms, pour in a splash of **Cognac** and set alight. When the flames subside, stir in a good couple of dashes of **double cream**, add a splash of **Tabasco sauce** and serve.

kidneys with garlic and wine

I just love kidneys. Veal kidneys are regarded as the finest, but lambs' kidneys are damned good. If you don't want to do it yourself, ask your butcher to remove the skin and the core.

Get some **kidneys**, remove the membrane that covers them, cut them in half and take out the little white core in the middle.

Get a couple of **shallots**, peel them and chop them very finely. Get a good handful of **parsley** and chop that up very finely, then peel a couple of **garlic cloves** and finely chop. Have ready a tablespoon of **tomato purée**, a good splash of **red wine** and some **Cognac**. Have ready a couple of slices of **bread**, already toasted or fried in **oil**.

Now, heat a good splash of oil in a pan and soften the garlic and the shallots, but do not let them burn. Flip in the kidneys, pour in a glass of Cognac and set alight. When the flames subside, stir in the tomato purée, splash in the red wine and cook very quickly, until the kidneys are tender. Season with lots of **black pepper**.

Serve on the bread and garnish with lots of chopped parsley.

poached eggs in red wine

This is a dish that may make Arnold Bennett turn in his grave, but it fortified the vignerons of Burgundy when they returned from a hard day, particularly in the winter, in the vineyards. It will be deep red and luscious in appearance.

Button mushrooms a handful of, chopped

Unsalted butter a good knob of

Bacon 2 rashers of, diced

Bread 4 slices of

Garlic 1 clove, peeled and crushed

Red wine a good ½ bottle

Water 1 litre/1¾ pints

Salt a big pinch of

Wine vinegar a good slosh of

Eggs 8

For the wine sauce

Unsalted butter a knob of

Bacon 2 rashers of, diced

Onion 1, peeled and chopped

Shallots 2 or 3, peeled and finely chopped

Garlic 1 clove, peeled and crushed

Carrots 2, peeled and finely chopped

Plain flour a large dash of

Good red wine 1 bottle

Bouquet garni 1 (fresh thyme, parsley stalks and 1 bay leaf, tied together with string)

Chicken stock 300 ml/10 fl oz

Salt and pepper

Serves 8

Begin by making the sauce. Heat the butter in a large heavy-based pan and brown the diced bacon with the onion, shallots, garlic and carrots. Then add a large dash of flour and stir it around until it is slightly coloured. Add the wine and bouquet garni and simmer, uncovered, until this has reduced by half.

Add the stock and stir again until everything is well mixed, then season with salt and pepper. Keep simmering and reducing until the sauce coats the spoon. Strain this into a bowl, discard the herbs and vegetables and set aside.

Next, fry the mushrooms in the butter until just giving off their juice. Add the bacon to the pan and brown, then lift both the bacon and mushrooms out of the pan and set aside.

Rub the slices of bread with the garlic and grill them. While you are doing that, put the wine, water, salt and vinegar into a pan and bring to the boil, then break the eggs into the liquid and poach for 3 minutes. Lift out with a slotted spoon and drain well.

Pour the wine sauce into bowls, place a poached egg in the sauce in each bowl and sprinkle over the browned mushrooms and bacon. Serve with the bread.

Many people have gas-fired barbecues, weird domed metal smokers, but you cannot beat a proper barbecue fuelled by charcoal.

We British are obsessed with barbecues – we invariably choose a day when it's bound to piss down with rain, then we cremate the burgers and undercook the sausages. This curious ritual is invariably orchestrated by the man of the house, wearing an ill-fitting or too small striped apron, a pair of tongs in one hand and a pint of lager in the other, while flames generated by the dripping fat lick round the unidentified frying objects. But, there is a better way. My way.

Kebabs can be prepared well in advance, fish can be cleaned and kept fresh in the fridge. Bowls of salad should be prepared well in advance, then wrapped in clingfilm and dressed at the last minute. If you are using charcoal, don't start to cook until the charcoal is covered with a fine white or grey powder. Flames should never be permitted to lick around the food. Do not attempt to barbecue food that is partly frozen or cold from the fridge, make sure it is removed from the fridge at least an hour before you are going to cook it. This will speed the cooking process wonderfully. Don't season the food with salt or pepper until it is sealed, otherwise you will draw out and lose the moisture and the flavours.

Do experiment with different foods, it is not necessary to have just burgers and sausages!

a good grilling

fish with lemon sauce

This can be a real party dish. The bigger the fish the better, but freshness is essential.

1 whole **fish, such as bream**, weighing about 1.75 kg/4 lb, gutted, fins trimmed but scales left on (this protects the fish while grilling)

Celery leaves a large bunch of

Lemon slices or wedges

Fresh parsley a handful of chopped

Olive oil a little

Salt and pepper

For the lemon sauce

Egg yolks 4

Eggs 2

Unsalted butter a good knob of

Plain flour 2 tablespoons

Lemon juice 300 ml/10 fl oz

Fresh mint 1 tablespoon chopped

Serves 4–6

Preheat the grill or have the barbecue ready. Stuff the fish with the celery leaves, lemon slices or wedges and parsley and season with salt and pepper in the cavity. Rub the outside of the fish with salt and oil, slap on the barbecue or under the grill and cook for 15 minutes each side.

While the fish is cooking, make the lemon sauce. Beat together the egg yolks and eggs. Melt the butter in a saucepan over a medium heat, add the flour and cook, stirring, until you have a smooth roux (paste). Over a medium heat, whisk in the lemon juice until you have a smooth sauce.

Remove the pan from the heat and allow to cool a little, then, whisking furiously, slowly pour in the beaten egg mixture. Continue to whisk like mad (off the heat) until the sauce thickens. Season and stir in the chopped mint.

Place the cooked fish on a serving dish, pour over the lemon sauce and serve.

barbecued
whole fish

For the last couple of moments of cooking, remove the foil and allow the scales to burn off, leaving a wonderfully crisp skin. It is the scales that protect the fish during cooking. You can use bream, bass, gurnard or very big grey mullets, it is your choice.

Make sure the **fish** are completely gutted, but do not scale them (the scales protect the fish while they are on the barbecue). Stuff the fish with slivers of **lemon** or **lime**, **thyme** sprigs and, if possible, sprigs of **fennel**. Baste the fish well with **olive oil** and wrap them loosely in cooking foil. Place on the barbecue and cook for 15–20 minutes on one side (depending on the size of your fish), then turn them over and cook for another 15–20 minutes.

To finish, remove the foil and place the fish back on the barbecue so the scales burn off.

Serve with a **hollandaise**, **anchovy** or **chilli sauce**, or **garlic mayonnaise**.

grilled fish with anchovy aïoli

It is perfectly OK to buy good-quality frozen fish fillets, but do allow them to defrost completely before cooking.

Garlic 4 cloves, peeled and finely chopped

Fresh parsley a good handful of chopped

Olive oil 2 tablespoons

Firm tomatoes 2 large, cut in half and deseeded

Unskinned fillets of cod or haddock 4 firm, trimmed neatly

Lemon juice of ½

Rustic bread, such as tomato, olive or focaccia 4 thick slices of

Salt and pepper

For the anchovy aïoli

Anchovy fillets in olive oil 50 g/2 oz can

Garlic 2 cloves, peeled and crushed

Eggs 3

Olive oil 300 ml/10 fl oz

To make the aïoli, place the anchovy fillets and garlic in a food processor and whiz to a paste. Keeping the food processor going, add the eggs, one at a time, and whiz until amalgamated with the anchovy and garlic. Keep whizzing while very slowly drizzling in the oil for a few seconds until you have a smooth mayonnaise. Season with salt and pepper and put aside.

Preheat the grill. Mix the garlic and parsley with a little of the oil and fill the tomato halves with this mixture. Set aside.

Brush the fish fillets on both sides with a little more oil and season with salt and pepper.

Heat a heavy-based frying pan and fry the fillets skin-side down for 2–3 minutes, then turn them over and cook for 2–3 minutes until they are cooked. Squeeze over the lemon juice and set aside in a warm place.

Sprinkle the bread slices on both sides with a little oil and grill on both sides until crispy and browned.

Using the same pan as you fried the fish in, lightly fry the stuffed tomatoes until just softened.

Place a slice of the toasted bread on a plate and put a fish fillet on top. Garnish the plate with the stuffed tomato, drizzle over the aïoli and serve.

red mullet with anchovy sauce

Absolutely one of my favourite fish. I would never discriminate between a mullet, a lobster or a plate of scallops. They are all fabulous.

Red mullet 4 medium-sized, whole, gutted and scales removed

Fennel seeds 1 teaspoon

Unsalted butter a large knob of

Olive oil a dash of

Salt and pepper

For the anchovy sauce

Unsalted butter 25 g/1 oz

Double cream 50 ml/2 fl oz

Anchovy essence 1 tablespoon

White sauce 600 ml/1 pint

Preheat the grill.

Season the cavity of each red mullet with salt and pepper, sprinkle in some fennel seeds and pop in a knob of butter. Sprinkle the fish with a dash of oil, then place under the grill and cook for about 5 minutes on each side, or until the fish is golden and the flesh is opaque and cooked. Set aside to keep warm.

Meanwhile, make the anchovy sauce. Add the butter, cream and anchovy essence to the white sauce and simmer for about 7 minutes, stirring all the time. Adjust the seasoning as necessary.

Place the fish on a serving dish, pour over the sauce and serve immediately.

fish with coriander and garlic

Make sure your fish is totally fresh and you have taken off the fins. I personally prefer to leave the head on, but some people are squeamish about that. If you do leave the head on, remove the gills as they can add a bitter taste.

Red mullet or mackerel 4, each about 275 g/10 oz, cleaned and gutted

Garlic 10 cloves, peeled and roughly chopped

Fresh coriander leaves and stalks a good handful of, chopped

Ground white pepper a pinch of

Vegetable oil a dash of

Salt

Chilli sauce bottled

Score each fish 3 or 4 times on each side to create slits.

Throw the garlic, chopped coriander, pepper, oil and salt to taste into a food processor and whiz to a paste. Rub this paste into the fish cavities and slits.

Wrap each fish individually in cooking foil and seal carefully, then leave in the fridge for 1 hour.

When your barbecue is hot, place the foil fish parcels on the barbecue and cook for 15 minutes on each side until the fish is fragrant and the flesh is cooked

Transfer on to serving dishes and serve with chilli sauce.

scallop kebab

Don't be afraid of using scallops, they are a delicate morsel but are protected and basted by the bacon, which should be crisp while the scallops are meltingly tender.

Take some **scallops** and wrap each of them in thin, **rindless streaky bacon**, then thread them onto a skewer and cook them on the barbecue for a minute or two.

Serve with freshly squeezed **lime juice** and, if you wish, a little bought **garlic mayonnaise**.

prawns in sea salt

Prawns are delicious this way. The thick sea salt crystallizes around the shells and adds a unique sweetness to the prawns, and you can eat the whole thing. However, you must use good-quality sea salt – table salt will not do. Whatever you do, don't peel them!

Fresh raw prawns, heads and shells on, or sardines 450 g/1 lb
Olive oil a splash of
Coarse sea salt a good handful of
Lemon juice freshly squeezed, to serve

If you are using wooden skewers, soak them in cold water overnight.

Sprinkle the prawns or sardines with a little oil, then roll them in plenty of sea salt until well covered – this will give a sweet, crunchy flavour.

Thread onto skewers, pop on the barbecue and cook for about 1 minute on each side.

Serve sprinkled with lemon juice.

prawns with chilli and coriander

Serve with small cubes of peeled and deseeded cucumber, chopped fresh mint and coriander and a jolly good squeeze of fresh lime juice.

Fresh raw prawns 350 g/12 oz, peeled and deveined

For the marinade

Fresh red chilli 1 long, deseeded and finely chopped

Garlic clove 1, peeled and very finely chopped

Soy sauce 2 teaspoons light

Oyster sauce 1 tablespoon

Fresh coriander leaves a handful of chopped

Lime juice of 1

Sesame oil a good dash

Vegetable oil a little

Ground white pepper a pinch

Combine all the ingredients for the marinade in a bowl. Add the prawns and mix well until they are all covered with the marinade, then cover and leave in the fridge overnight, turning occasionally. If you are using wooden skewers, you will need to soak them in cold water overnight.

Lift the prawns out of the marinade and thread onto skewers.

Pop onto the barbecue, brush on a little of the marinade and cook for 6–8 minutes on each side, basting with the marinade. The prawns will turn pink when they are cooked.

tuna kebabs

The cubes of firm, fresh tuna should be seared on the outside and slightly pink on the inside. To test if they are cooked, press down on the fish – if it is firm, it is ready. Don't overcook tuna – it is better a little underdone as the marinade will have slightly 'cooked' the fish.

Fresh tuna 1 kg/2¼ lb piece of

Lemon wedges, to serve

For the marinade

Ground cinnamon 1 teaspoon

Ground cumin 1 teaspoon

Ground sweet paprika 1 teaspoon

Ground coriander 1 teaspoon

Fresh parsley ½ cup chopped

Coriander leaves ½ cup chopped fresh

Lemon juice ½ cup

Olive oil a good dash

Grated lemon rind 1 teaspoon

Serves 6

Cut the tuna into 3.5 cm/1½ inch cubes. Combine all the marinade ingredients in a large bowl and mix well.

Add the tuna to the marinade and mix well so that all the tuna is coated in the marinade, then cover and leave in the fridge overnight. If you are using wooden skewers, soak them in cold water overnight.

The next day, thread the tuna onto 8 skewers.

Grill on the barbecue for about 3 minutes each side and serve with lemon wedges.

kidney kebabs

The flavour of this delicious offal will be enhanced if you can buy the kidneys still surrounded by their fat. Bacon goes well with any offal and it will also help to keep the kidneys basted while they are cooking.

Lambs' kidneys 8, skin and core removed, cut in half

Streaky bacon 8 rashers of, cut in half

Courgettes 2, cut into 2.5 cm/1 inch pieces

Red onions 2, peeled and cut into quarters

Olive oil for brushing

For the marinade

Ground cumin 2 teaspoons

Sweet paprika 4 teaspoons

Chilli powder ½ teaspoon

Lime juice of 1

Olive oil a good splash of

Salt and pepper

If you are using wooden skewers, soak them in cold water overnight.

Mix all the ingredients for the marinade in a large bowl. Throw in the kidneys and coat with the marinade, then leave for 20–25 minutes.

Wrap each kidney in half a rasher of bacon and thread onto the skewers, alternating a kidney, a piece of courgette and a piece of onion.

Brush the kebabs with plenty of oil, then barbecue them for 3–4 minutes on each side until they are cooked.

Serve immediately with a salad or dip of your choice.

lamb kebabs

This is very much a spring dish and you should use the youngest, freshest lamb that you can find. If you want to reduce the heat factor slightly, deseed the chilli. It is better to have the lamb slightly rare, particularly with young, tender lamb.

Lamb fillet 1 kg/2¼ lb boneless, cut into 3.5 cm/1½ inch cubes

For the marinade

Large onions 2, peeled and finely chopped

Garlic 2 cloves, peeled and finely chopped

Olive oil a good splash of

Lemons juice of 2

Ground cumin 1 teaspoon

Ground coriander 1 teaspoon

Ground ginger ½ teaspoon

For the tomato sauce

Chopped tomatoes 400 g/13 oz can

Red chilli 1 small, finely chopped

Ground cumin ½ teaspoon

Ground cinnamon ¼ teaspoon

Olive oil a dash of

Serves 6

Mix all the marinade ingredients together in a bowl, then add the lamb and stir well to coat the meat. Cover the bowl and place in the fridge overnight. If you are using wooden skewers, soak them in cold water overnight.

The next day, remove the lamb from the bowl and put to one side, then scrape the marinade ingredients into a food processor and blitz. Sieve into a pan.

Place all the ingredients for the tomato sauce into the pan with the sieved marinade ingredients and simmer for 5–8 minutes, stirring well.

Thread the lamb onto skewers and cook on the barbecue for about 5 minutes on each side until done as you like it.

Serve with the tomato sauce on the side.

minced lamb kebabs

If possible, use a boned half shoulder of lamb with lots of fat in it as it is cheaper and has more flavour. Preferably, it should be minced by hand, not in a food processor.

Minced lamb 750 g/1½ lb

Large onion 1, peeled and grated

Garlic 2 cloves, peeled and finely minced

Cloves ¼ teaspoon ground

Nutmeg ¼ teaspoon ground

Hot paprika ¼ teaspoon ground

Ground cumin ½ teaspoon

Ground coriander ½ teaspoon

Lemon rind 1 teaspoon finely grated

Pine nuts ¼ cup, finely chopped

Fresh parsley a good handful of chopped

Olive oil for brushing

Lemon wedges, to serve

Serves 4–6

In a large bowl, combine the lamb, onion, garlic, spices and lemon rind and mix very well. Add the nuts and parsley and mix well, then cover and put in the fridge overnight. If you are using wooden skewers, soak them in cold water overnight.

The next day, using your hands, make little oval rolls of the minced lamb and thread onto skewers, about three per skewer. Brush with oil on both sides.

Pop on the barbecue until well browned and cooked through.

Serve with lemon wedges.

lamb kofte

You could use fresh mint in this dish, but I find it works best with dried mint, which has a more intense flavour. Serve this with a dip of natural yoghurt and chopped, fresh mint.

Minced lamb 1 kg/2¼ lb

Dried mint a good sprinkling

Olive oil a dash

Salt and pepper

Serves 6

If you are using wooden skewers, soak them in cold water overnight.

Put the lamb in a bowl, add the mint and salt and pepper to taste and sprinkle on a little oil. Form into small patties, about 3.5 cm/1½ inches wide.

Thread onto skewers, place on the barbecue and cook until all sides are browned and sealed.

tikka kebab

Adding yogurt to this dish does help to tenderize the meat a little. It will blacken on cooking and add a crust to the kebab, but this is how it should be.

Natural yoghurt 150 ml/5 fl oz

Red onions 4 small, peeled and quartered

Garlic 3 cloves, peeled and finely chopped

Ground turmeric ½ teaspoon

White wine vinegar 1 tablespoon

Boned lamb shoulder or leg 450 g/1 lb, cut into 2.5 cm/1 inch cubes

Lemon juice of 1

Green pepper 1, deseeded and cut into 2.5 cm/1 inch squares

Salt and pepper

Lemon wedges, to garnish

Put the yogurt, half the onions, the garlic, turmeric, vinegar and salt and pepper to taste in a bowl and mix well.

Sprinkle the lamb with the lemon juice and mix well, then add the lamb to the yogurt mixture and stir well. Cover the bowl and leave overnight in the fridge. If you are using wooden skewers, soak them in cold water overnight.

Thread the meat onto the skewers, alternating meat, a piece of onion and a piece of green pepper until you have used up all of the ingredients.

Cook on the barbecue, turning frequently until the lamb is cooked through.

Serve garnished with lemon wedges.

beef kebabs

I recommend some nice, well-hung, well-marbled fillet of beef for this one. Serve with some freshly made, freshly grated horseradish mixed with double cream and a dash of white wine vinegar.

Cut some **fillet of beef** into 2.5 cm/1 inch squares. Cut some deseeded **red peppers** to the same size. Cut some **pork fat** to the same size. Thread them all alternately onto skewers (pre-soaked if wooden) and pop on the barbecue for a few minutes, depending on how you like your beef cooked. Serve with some bought **anchovy sauce**.

pork kebabs

An Asian twist to a British meat. The marinade will add a depth of flavour to the pork. Do not be tempted to use fillet or similar lean meat, since you need the flavour of the fat from the shoulder. The addition of a little sugar will help to slightly caramelize the pork, further enhancing the flavour.

Cut a boned **shoulder** or **leg of pork** into 2.5 cm/1 inch cubes.

In a large bowl, mix 5 tablespoons **soy sauce**, 1 tablespoon chopped **fresh root ginger**, 4 tablespoons **medium sherry**, a pinch of **ground star anise**, 1 tablespoon **caster sugar** to make a marinade. Add the pork cubes and mix well to make sure all the pork is coated. Cover and leave in the fridge overnight. If you are using wooden skewers, soak them in cold water overnight.

Thread the pork cubes onto skewers and grill for about 20 minutes, turning frequently until they are golden and cooked through. Serve with a light sauce or dip of your choice.

chicken kebabs

The spicy chicken in these kebabs is a perfect foil for the sweet, soft prunes. Fruit and meat always go well together. The alcohol you use is up to you – brandy, Madeira or port will all really stand up in this dish.

Cut some skinless, **boneless chicken breasts** into cubes and marinate overnight in **lime juice** and **chilli sauce**.

Soak some **stoned prunes** in **alcohol**, then wrap tightly in **rindless streaky bacon**. Thread the chicken and prunes alternately onto skewers (pre-soaked if wooden) and cook on the barbecue for a few minutes on each side until the chicken is cooked through.

charcoal pork and beef

A delicious mix of sweet and savoury. You must use pork belly for this as the flavour is incomparable and it is very forgiving when slapped on the barbecue.

For the caramel sauce

Caster sugar ⅓ cup

Fish sauce a generous splash of

Shallots 4 , peeled and finely sliced

Pepper

For the kebab

Minced beef 450 g/1 lb

Garlic 8 cloves, peeled and grated

Fresh pork belly 450 g/1 lb, cut into 5 mm/¼ inch slices about 5 cm/2 inches long

Serves 6

If you are using wooden skewers, soak them in cold water overnight.

To make the caramel sauce, place the sugar in a heavy-based saucepan over a low heat and keep swirling the pan (not stirring) until the sugar melts and turns brown. The minute all the sugar has dissolved, remove from the heat and stir in the fish sauce. Return the pan to the heat and cook for another minute or two, then throw in the shallots and black pepper, stir well and set aside.

Place the minced beef and garlic in a large bowl, stir in half the caramel sauce and blend well. Place the pork belly and the remaining caramel sauce in another bowl and mix well. Leave both to stand for about 30 minutes.

Form the beef mince into small, 3.5 cm/1½ inch balls and thread onto skewers (about 4 pieces to a skewer) until you have used up all the meat. Do the same with the pork slices (do not mix the meats on the skewers as they take different times to cook).

Place the pork skewers on the grill and cook for 10–15 minutes, turning frequently until nicely browned, then add the beef skewers, which will take about 4–5 minutes each side.

barbecued
spareribs

Make sure you have lots of finger bowls, plenty of paper napkins and enjoy. This is fine finger food, sticky and full of flavour. It is also delicious when eaten cold.

Caramel sauce 1 quantity (see page 71)

Fresh lemon grass 2 stalks, woody part discarded, the rest chopped up

Shallots 4, peeled

Red chilli 1 large, fresh, deseeded

Garlic 4 cloves, peeled

Spareribs 900 g/2 lb, cut into individual ribs

Prepare the caramel sauce and set aside to cool.

Put the lemon grass, shallots, chilli and garlic into a food processor and whiz to a paste. Stir this paste into the cooled caramel sauce.

Put the ribs into a shallow dish, pour over the caramel mixture and turn the ribs well to make sure they are all coated, then leave in the fridge for at least 2 hours.

When your barbecue is hot, drain the spareribs, reserving the marinade for basting, and cook on the barbecue, basting frequently with the marinade, until crisp, golden and nicely glazed.

Asian-style chicken kebabs

Chicken can be quite bland, but these ingredients add a real Asian tang without overwhelming the subtle taste of the chicken. Where possible, buy free-range chicken and make sure it is well cooked.

Skinless chicken breast fillets 1 kg/2¼ lb, cut into 3.5 x 10 cm/1½ x 4 inch strips

For the marinade

Red shallots 3, peeled and chopped

Garlic 4 cloves, peeled and chopped

Coriander roots 4, chopped

Fresh root ginger 2.5 cm/1 inch piece of, peeled and chopped

Coriander seeds 1 tablespoon

Cumin seeds 1 tablespoon

Ground turmeric 1 tablespoon

Curry powder 1 teaspoon

Light soy sauce 2 tablespoons

Coconut milk 400 ml/14 fl oz can

Vegetable oil 4 tablespoons

Demerara or palm sugar 2 tablespoons

Salt 1 teaspoon

Serves 6

If you are using wooden skewers, soak them in cold water overnight.

In a food processor, whiz the shallots, garlic, coriander roots and ginger to a paste, then tip into a bowl.

Dry-fry the coriander seeds, cumin seeds and turmeric until they release their aroma, then grind to a powder in a spice grinder. Add the ground spices to the garlic paste along with the curry powder, soy sauce, coconut milk, oil, sugar and salt and mix well.

Add the chicken to the marinade, mixing well to make sure that all the chicken is well coated, then cover and leave to marinate in the fridge for at least 6 hours, turning every so often.

Thread the chicken strips onto the skewers lengthways and grill for 10 minutes on each side, or until the chicken is cooked and slightly blackened.

Serve hot with satay sauce.

vegetable kebabs

You do not have to follow my suggestion for vegetables, use what you have or what you like best.

Olive oil a good splash of

Mixed dried herbs, such as rosemary, thyme, oregano

Onions, peeled and quartered

Aubergines, trimmed and cut into large chunks

Cherry tomatoes a large handful of

Red or green peppers, deseeded and cut into chunks

Courgettes, cut into 2.5 cm/1 inch chunks

Salt and pepper

If you are using wooden skewers, soak them in cold water overnight.

Pour a good splash of oil into a flat dish, then add the herbs and salt and pepper to taste.

Thread alternate vegetables onto each skewer – a piece of onion, aubergine, tomato, pepper, etc. – to make a colourful mix. Marinate the skewers in the oil mixture, turning occasionally, for about 1 hour.

When your barbecue is hot, cook the vegetable kebabs, turning occasionally, until the vegetables are golden and tender.

getting a roasting

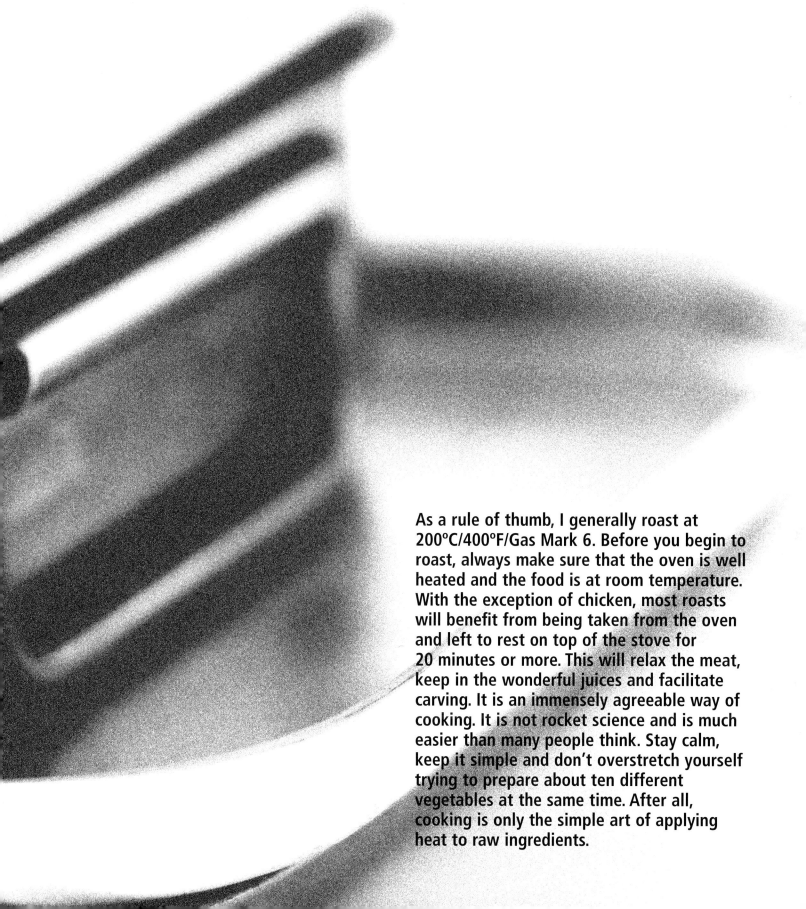

As a rule of thumb, I generally roast at 200°C/400°F/Gas Mark 6. Before you begin to roast, always make sure that the oven is well heated and the food is at room temperature. With the exception of chicken, most roasts will benefit from being taken from the oven and left to rest on top of the stove for 20 minutes or more. This will relax the meat, keep in the wonderful juices and facilitate carving. It is an immensely agreeable way of cooking. It is not rocket science and is much easier than many people think. Stay calm, keep it simple and don't overstretch yourself trying to prepare about ten different vegetables at the same time. After all, cooking is only the simple art of applying heat to raw ingredients.

herring with apples

Sadly, the herring has been overfished, but its wonderful, oily flesh makes a perfect candidate for stuffing and baking. Once the food of the working classes, it is now something of the piscatorial exotica.

Herring 4 large, cleaned

Onion 1 small, peeled and finely chopped

Dessert apples 225 g/8 oz, peeled, cored and grated

Caster sugar 1 teaspoon

White breadcrumbs 75 g/3 oz

Unsalted butter 50 g/2 oz melted, plus butter for greasing

Salt and pepper

Preheat the oven to 220°C/425°F/Gas Mark 7.

First bone the fish. Cut the herring along the belly and place belly-side down on a board. Push down on the backbone, then turn the fish over, pull out the backbone from the cavity side and cut the backbone off at the head.

Mix the onion with the apple, sugar and two-thirds of the breadcrumbs, then season to taste. Stuff the herrings with this mixture and lay them in a buttered ovenproof dish.

Scatter the remaining breadcrumbs over the herrings, pour over half the melted butter and bake in the oven for about 20 minutes.

Pour the remaining melted butter over the herrings just before serving.

potted shrimps

There was no trip to the seaside, in my long-distant youth, when the two greatest treats were not a tub of potted shrimps followed by a Devon double-cream ice-cream wafer. Where have all the wafers gone?

Shrimps 450 g/1 lb fresh, raw, shells on

Clarified butter 150 g/5 oz

Anchovy essence 2 teaspoons

Mace ¼ teaspoon

Cayenne pepper ¼ teaspoon

Salt

Preheat the oven to 180°C/350°F/Gas Mark 4.

Put the shrimps into a large saucepan of boiling water and cook for a couple of minutes, or until the shrimps just turn pink. Drain and leave to cool, then remove from their shells and place in an ovenproof dish.

Melt just over half of the clarified butter and mix in the anchovy essence, mace, cayenne pepper and salt to taste. Pour this over the shrimps and bake in the oven for 30 minutes.

Remove the shrimps from the oven, strain the cooking liquid into a bowl and reserve. Put the shrimps aside to cool.

When cool, divide the shrimps between several ramekin dishes and pour over the cooking liquid. Leave to set, then melt the remaining clarified butter, pour over the top and chill until required.

sea bass stuffed with rice and dates

You might consider this a curious concoction, but I can assure you the novelty is definitely worth the effort and there are many who say that it is the bass and not the salmon that is the king of fish.

Limes juice of 2

Sea bass 1 whole, 900 g–1.4 kg/2–3 lb, gutted, fins and scales removed

Dates 1½ cups of chopped

Crystallized ginger 4 pieces of, finely chopped

Almonds 2 tablespoons blanched, finely chopped

Rice 2 cups of cooked

Ground cinnamon 1 teaspoon

Unsalted butter 50 g/2 oz cold, cut into cubes, plus extra for greasing

Salt and pepper

Butter melted, to serve

Lime wedges, to garnish

Serves 4–6

Preheat the oven to 220°C/425°F/Gas Mark 7.

Sprinkle the lime juice into the fish cavity and season with salt and pepper. Mix the dates with the ginger, almonds, rice and cinnamon and stir in most of the butter cubes. Stuff the fish with the mixture, then place the fish on a large piece of buttered cooking foil and sprinkle the remaining butter cubes over the fish.

Wrap the foil quite tightly around the fish, place on a baking tray and bake in the oven for about 40 minutes.

Unwrap the fish, place on a serving dish and pour over some melted butter. Garnish with the lime wedges and serve.

bream fillet parcels

Bream is a very delicately flavoured fish so take care not to overcook it. As I frequently say, the enjoyment of cooking relies on sourcing brilliant ingredients and applying culinary common sense.

Olive oil for brushing

Courgettes 2, cut into thin discs

Tomatoes 2, thinly sliced

Unsalted butter a large knob of, plus extra for greasing

Bream 4 fillets of

Shallot 1, peeled and finely chopped

Bay leaves 4

Fresh thyme 4 sprigs of

Fresh parsley a handful of chopped

Good fish stock 4 tablespoons

Dry white wine 1 wine glass

Salt and pepper

Preheat the oven to 220°C/425°F/Gas Mark 7. Cut four pieces of cooking foil into 25–30 cm/10–12 inch squares, lay them flat and brush one side of each with oil.

Put the courgettes and tomatoes in a buttered ovenproof dish and bake in the oven for about 10 minutes until softening.

Place a fillet of bream on each piece of greased foil and season with salt and pepper. Place some shallot, 1 bay leaf, 1 sprig of thyme and a little chopped parsley on each fillet. Divide the courgette and tomato into four portions and lay these on top of the fish, then sprinkle a splash of fish stock and a dash of wine over each portion and dot with butter.

Pull up the sides of the foil around the fish to form a tight seal, but allow room in the parcel for steam to form. Put on a baking tray and cook in the oven for 7–8 minutes.

Serve the fish sealed in their parcels. The aromas and flavours are revealed when the parcels are cut open at the table.

roasted
monkfish

The BBC, several hundred years ago, made a programme called *Floyd On Fish*. At that time, monkfish was despised by all except the Italians, who made so-called scampi from it. But it has to be one of the finest fish, despite its ugliness, and is ideal for roasting, and after that TV series it became immensely popular.

Monkfish tail 1, about 900 g/2 lb, skinned and backbone removed to produce two good fillets

Lemon juice of ½

Fresh parsley a small handful of finely chopped

Garlic 2 cloves, peeled and finely chopped

Butter for greasing

Onions 8–10 small whole, peeled and sautéed in butter and oil until golden

Smoked bacon 50 g/2 oz, diced

Dry white wine 1 wine glass

Double cream 150 ml/5 fl oz

Salt and pepper

Preheat the oven to 200°C/400°F/Gas Mark 6. Season the monkfish fillets with salt, pepper and the lemon juice. Sprinkle the parsley and garlic over one of the fillets, place the other fillet on top and tie the two fillets together with string, sandwiching the flavourings between.

Place the fish in a buttered roasting tray with the onions and bacon and roast in the oven for 30 minutes.

Remove the roasting tray from the oven, turn the fish over and add the wine to the tray, then return to the oven and roast for another 15 minutes.

Remove from the oven, take out the fish, onions and bacon and place on a warm serving dish.

Put the roasting tray over a low heat on the hob, stir the cream into the cooking juices and heat through, then strain the sauce over the fish. Serve immediately

fish in filo pastry with pernod sauce

Aniseed and fish go together like a horse and carriage, so this is a smart little number and now that filo pastry is so easy to acquire, why not try it?

Unsalted butter 125 g/4 oz

Sultanas 4 tablespoons chopped

Firm fish, such as sea bass, salmon or similar 4 thick fillets of, skinned

Lemon 4 slices of

Mint leaves a handful of fresh

Filo pastry 16 sheets of

Salt and pepper

For the sauce

Butter a knob of

Plain flour 1 heaped tablespoon

Pernod or pastis 1 wine glass

Egg yolks 2, beaten

Fresh mint 1 tablespoon chopped

Preheat the oven to 220°C/425°F/Gas Mark 7. To prepare the fish, melt half the butter and put to one side.

Scatter the sultanas over two of the fish fillets, then place the lemon slices on the sultanas and then the mint leaves on top of the lemons. Season with salt and pepper and place a knob of butter in the middle of each fillet. Place the two remaining fillets on the top to create a 'sandwich'.

Lay out a sheet of filo pastry and brush with the melted butter, then place the fillet 'sandwich' in the middle of the pastry and neatly wrap with the pastry. Continue to add buttered filo pastry until you have at least four layers of pastry to each parcel.

Brush the pastry again with butter and place the parcels on a baking sheet. Bake in the oven for 12–15 minutes until the pastry is golden brown.

While the fish is in the oven, make the sauce. Melt the butter in a saucepan over a medium heat, add the flour and stir well until you have a smooth roux (paste). Cook the roux for a couple of minutes, stirring all the time, then whisk in the Pernod or pastis until you have a smooth sauce. Remove the pan from the heat and allow to cool a little, then whisk in the egg yolks until the sauce thickens. Add the chopped mint and season with salt and pepper to taste.

To serve, pour the sauce over the bottom of a serving dish and place the fish parcels on the top.

mackerel with gooseberries

What childhood holiday was complete without a mackerel fishing trip in the bay? Like the herring, its oily and firm flesh can be brilliantly flavoured with these gorgeous gooseberries, which, in my childhood, grew in every garden.

Plump mackerel 4, gutted and washed under a cold tap

Unsalted butter 50 g/2 oz, plus extra for greasing

Salt and pepper

For the sauce

Fresh gooseberries 225 g/8 oz, topped and tailed

Caster sugar 25 g/1 oz

Unsalted butter 25 g/1 oz

Nutmeg a pinch of freshly grated

Preheat the oven to 180°C/350°F/Gas Mark 4.

Place the mackerel in a buttered ovenproof dish, season with salt and pepper and dot with the butter. Cover the dish with cooking foil and bake in the oven for about 30 minutes.

While the fish is cooking, make the sauce. Put the gooseberries in a pan with a little water and simmer until they are tender.

Pass the gooseberries through a sieve set over the pan to remove any seeds or skin. Beat in the sugar and butter and season with nutmeg, salt and pepper. Heat through gently.

To serve, take the mackerel out of the oven, remove the fillets from the backbone and place on a serving dish. Pour over the gooseberry sauce and serve.

roast chicken with garlic

Yes, I am serious about the quantity of garlic. When garlic is cooked, it becomes mild and creamy, not ferocious as it is raw. Use young garlic if you can get it, but if not, always remove the green shoot from inside as this is bitter.

Buy one very large, plump corn-fed, **free-range chicken**, and while you are shopping for that, buy 1 kg/2¼ lb of very fat **garlic heads** (and I do mean a kilo). Also, get a big bunch of **fresh thyme** and 3 **lemons**, and make sure you have some **olive oil** at home.

This dish is so simple, but is outrageously delicious and should be served with a crispy **green salad** and some freshly cooked **green beans**, so don't forget to buy them as well.

So, first of all make sure your oven is at 200°C/400°F/Gas Mark 6. Take the papery skins off the heads of garlic, but don't peel the cloves. Cut one lemon into quarters and stuff it into the cavity of the chicken with the thyme and as many cloves of garlic as you can manage. I must emphasize that the garlic cloves should be the fat ones, not the mean, thin supermarket things you can get.

Put all the remaining garlic into a roasting tray and place a trivet over them so that the chicken can sit on the trivet. Rub the chicken all round with the juice of a second lemon, some olive oil and sea salt and place it, breast-side down, on the trivet. Save the third lemon for squeezing over the finished dish. Pour a good splash of olive oil and a little dash of water into the bottom of the roasting tray, then cover the lot with cooking foil and pop into the oven.

After about 1 hour, take out the roasting tray, remove the foil and turn the chicken on to its back, baste it once again with some olive oil, return it to the oven and let it cook until the skin is crispy and golden – up to another hour depending on the size of your chicken.

Once the chicken is cooked, take it out of the oven and squeeze the juice from the remaining lemon over it. Discard the lemon quarters from the cavity, carve the chicken and serve it with the plump, golden-roasted cloves of garlic, which will be like creamy chestnuts.

roast chicken with
tarragon sauce

Now this is a bit of a rich, buttery one. But as long as you don't eat it every day, it will do you no harm. Tarragon is a herb that is made to go with chicken, but do not overdo it as it is quite powerful.

Shop for a small, plump, corn-fed, **free-range chicken**, several branches of **fresh tarragon leaves**, a sprig of **thyme** and a good, plump **head of garlic**. Make sure you have available 4 **free-range eggs**, 350 g/12 oz of **unsalted butter**, 2 **lemons** and **white wine vinegar**.

Stuff the chicken with the thyme, a big knob of butter, one of the lemons cut into pieces and a good stalk of tarragon, then season the chicken thoroughly with lemon juice and sea salt. Remove all the other tarragon leaves from the stalks, chop finely and marinate them in a dash of the white wine vinegar.

Preheat the oven to 200°C/400°F/Gas Mark 6. Place the chicken in a roasting tray, rub it well with butter and put all the rest of the butter in the roasting tray. Roast the bird, breast-side down, in the oven for about 1 hour, basting it with melted butter from time to time. Then turn the chicken breast-side up to crisp the skin, baste again and continue to roast. Once the chicken is cooked – up to 1 hour more depending on the size of the chicken – remove it from the roasting tray and tip out any juices that may be in its cavity back into the roasting tray. Strain the juices and melted butter through a fine sieve into a suitable saucepan. Set the chicken aside to rest.

Now, separate the yolks from 4 eggs (keep the whites in the fridge for another day) and beat them together. Over a very gentle heat, whisk the egg yolks into the strained buttery juices and whisk hard until you have a thin, custard-like consistency. At this stage, whisk in the chopped tarragon leaves and the little bit of vinegar and continue to cook until warmed through. This must be done very delicately or else the whole thing will curdle.

Joint or carve the chicken and serve with this heart-attacking delicious butter and egg sauce.

roast pheasant with apple and cream sauce

This is an old-fashioned recipe and I suppose I am an old-fashioned cook. Pheasant is perfectly easy to cook, but keep your eye on it since it is not a fatty bird and will dry out if it is overcooked. This is a dish you can easily prepare the day before.

You need to shop for a very plump young **pheasant** (or two), half a dozen thin rashers of **fatty, streaky bacon**, a bottle of **dry white wine**, some **Demerara sugar**, a handful of **raisins or sultanas**, an **onion** and a **carrot**, 4 medium-sized **eating apples** and a bunch of **watercress**. I assume you will have **unsalted butter** in the fridge, and you will also need a small tub of **double cream** and a small jar of **apple compote**.

Peel the onion and carrot and chop both finely. Heat a large knob of butter in a casserole and fry the onion and carrot until they are softened and golden. Add the giblets, feet and neck of the pheasant, cover with wine and simmer gently for 1 hour or so.

Meanwhile, make sure the oven is at 200°C/400°F/Gas Mark 6. Wrap the pheasant in the streaky bacon, place it on a trivet in a roasting tray and pour a couple of dashes of (whoops, I forgot to mention) **dry cider** into the roasting tray. Cover the bird with cooking foil and roast in the oven for about 1 hour, checking it from time to time.

Once the pheasant is cooked, take out the roasting tray and empty any juices from the bird's cavity back into the tray. Set the pheasant aside to cool. Pour all the juices in the tray into your casserole of white wine and giblets.

Once the pheasant has cooled, quarter it and cut out the backbone. You can cover the pheasant pieces and pop in the fridge until the next day, if you like. Reduce the wine and juices in the casserole to about one-third of their original quantity and then strain. Put in a jug, cover and place in the fridge overnight.

We will use the same trick as for the Roast duck with kumquats (see page 93). Just before serving, heat 1 litre/ 1¾ pints of chicken stock and dump the pheasant joints into that to warm through. Then place under the grill for 5 minutes or so to crisp up the skin. Of course, do not discard the chicken stock – with a bit of vermicelli, some chillies and spring onions it will make a lovely broth for the next day.

Cut the apples in half and take out the pips, then stuff them with the sultanas. Sprinkle over some Demerara sugar and a knob of butter and arrange them around the pheasant so that you can grill the pheasant (until heated through) and the apple pieces at the same time.

While the pheasant is grilling, reheat the reduced sauce and, over a low heat, stir in some double cream and some of the apple compote to taste. Season with **salt** and **pepper** and, if you happen to have some **fresh nutmeg**, grate that in at the same time.

Arrange the pheasant on a serving dish, pour over the sauce and garnish with the stuffed apples and some spicy, peppery watercress.

roast duck with kumquats or oranges

This is a stylish dish and remarkably easy to make. You can even do most of the work the day before. Duck with orange seems very 1970s, but the flavours do work. Kumquats have a more tart flavour than oranges, so I leave the choice of which to use to you.

Because I see the roast duck with rich gravy in the recipe on page 95 very much as a Sunday lunch dish, I see my roast duck with kumquats very much as a dinner dish. Therefore, the best way to go is to cook the whole lot the day before your dinner party so you have minimum work to do on the day.

Firstly, you have to do a little extra shopping because, aside from the **duck**, you need to find a **vanilla pod**, a stick of **cinnamon**, some **Grand Marnier** and some **kumquats** (or you can use peeled orange segments). If you cannot find a vanilla pod, use a little real vanilla extract. Now, remember, this is a day-before cooking operation, which will take away all the pressure of your dinner party. So, prepare the gravy in exactly the same way as for the roast duck on page 95, but using **dry white wine** – don't forget when the duck has come out of the oven to tip all the juices from the duck cavity into the gravy. Then, cook to reduce the gravy to at least half its original volume.

Now, here is the cunning thing: once the duck or ducks are cold, joint them by cutting down through the middle – personally I think half a duck per person is reasonable, but if you are being mean cut it into quarters. Using poultry shears, cut out the backbone and discard it. Then, neatly joint the bird. Wrap the pieces of duck and put into the fridge.

Meanwhile, strain your reduced white wine and giblet gravy and put that in the fridge, too, so that the next day any fat that has floated to the top (and there will be fat) can be scooped off.

Once you have taken off the fat from the gravy, return the gravy to a pan and reduce it even further, then whack in the whole kumquats or orange segments, a splash of Grand Marnier, the cinnamon stick and vanilla pod. (You might also quite like to add a teaspoon or two of caster sugar.) Take off the heat and cool, then cover and put the gravy back in the fridge, and that will be ready to go when you are.

I forgot to tell you to buy some **chicken stock cubes** as you need a couple of litres, or 3½ pints, of chicken stock, because what you do on the night, to avoid minimum stress while you are cooking and hopefully having a splash yourself, is to heat the grill of the oven and heat the chicken stock in a saucepan. You dunk the duck joints into the stock just to warm through (the stock, by the way, will make nice soup the next day with the addition of a few veg), pop the ducks under the grill to get crisp, heat the kumquat sauce (remove the cinnamon stick and vanilla pod before serving) and hey, bingo, we are back somewhere in the 1970s. Quite frankly, who wants a rare *maigret de canard*? I certainly don't!

roast duck with a rich red wine gravy

Ask your butcher for a Gressingham duck – they are the best, and make sure he gives you the giblets.

Buy a first-class, **free-range duck** complete with its neck and giblets. Make sure you have a good bottle of **red wine**, some **dry sherry**, an **onion** or two and a **carrot** or two (both peeled and very finely diced), a clove or two of **garlic**, crushed, a splash of **olive oil**, some sprigs of **thyme** and **rosemary**, a **bay leaf**, a few **peppercorns** and a couple of **oranges** and **lemons**.

Now, the very clever thing about this recipe is you sauté the onions, carrots and garlic in olive oil in a casserole until they are soft, tender and slightly brown. Then you add a sprig of thyme, the bay leaf and peppercorns. Next, you stir in the giblets, the heart, liver and neck and stir them around. Then pour in the bottle of red wine and let it simmer away for at least 1 hour, after which time you can stir in ½ tablespoon of **tomato purée** (forgot to mention that) and a glass of dry sherry. But, the secret of enjoying a roast duck is to cook this gravy the day before you intend to cook the duck.

Now, the duck needs to be stuffed with sprigs of fresh thyme and rosemary and some lemon and orange quarters. It needs to be pricked all over and rubbed lightly in sea salt, then placed breast-side down on a trivet in a roasting tray, with a little water in the roasting tray. Make sure the oven is set at about 200°C/400°F/Gas Mark 6 and cook the bird for about 1 hour, then turn the duck over so that its breast can brown. Keep an eye on it.

Carefully tip any juices out of the duck cavity back into the roasting tray, then transfer the duck to a warm place and leave it to rest. Strain any juices from the roasting tray into the casserole of gravy you cooked the previous day, bubble up the gravy furiously and allow it to reduce to about half its original volume. Strain it through a fine sieve into a saucepan.

You can serve this dish with roast potatoes and apple sauce, plus a veg of your choice, whereas, with my dinner party duck on page 93, you will probably start the evening with a salad of crunchy leaves with a simple olive oil dressing, followed by the duck, some fine cheeses and some exquisite dessert (but I don't do desserts!).

roast loin of venison with black cherry sauce

This is a very rich dish, but because loin of venison is lean, it is easy to carve and can feed a lot of people in a very tasty fashion. I love fruit sauces with game and this is a favourite of mine.

Buy a beautiful piece of **boned loin of venison**, but make sure the butcher gives you the bones chopped up. Buy a **carrot**, an **onion**, some **thyme**, a **bay leaf**, 1 kg/2¼ lb of fresh **cherries** and make sure you have got some **cherry brandy** in your cocktail cabinet and some **red wine**. Also get some very thin rashers of **fatty, streaky bacon** so that you can wrap the loin of venison in it before you roast it.

Because venison does not take very long to roast, you can happily cook it in the oven on the day that you want to eat it, but the day before, in a separate casserole, brown your chopped onion and carrots in a little oil and butter, add the venison bones, a sprig of thyme and a bay leaf and pour in half a bottle of red wine to cover. Bring to the boil, then simmer until you have a rich gravy, then strain it and pop into the fridge until required. At the same time, stone all the cherries and put them into the sauce.

To roast your venison, preheat the oven to 200°C/400°F/ Gas Mark 6. Wrap the venison in the bacon, then put it on a trivet in a roasting tin and add a splash of water to the tin. Roast for about 30 minutes – it does not take long, just prod with a fork occasionally to see how it is getting on.

Meanwhile, all you have to do is add a good dash of cherry brandy and lots of coarsely **crushed black pepper** to your sauce and cook gently until the cherries begin to disintegrate.

Remove the venison from the oven and discard the bacon, then allow it to rest for 10 minutes or so. Carve the meat and place on a serving dish, then pour over your sauce.

roast fillet of beef with spicy butter

Ask your butcher for the middle cut of a well-marbled fillet and freeze the 'head and the tail' for kebabs another time.

Fillet of beef 900 g/2 lb piece of

Streaky bacon 350 g/12 oz rashers of

Garlic 2 heads of, cut in half across the entire middle of the head

Olive oil a sprinkling of

Salt and pepper

Fresh parsley a handful of chopped, to garnish

For the spicy butter

Fresh red pepper 1 large, roasted, skin and seeds removed

Fresh red chilli 1 large, roasted, skin and seeds removed

Anchovy fillets 3

Unsalted butter 275 g/10 oz at room temperature

Chilli powder a good pinch of

Parmesan cheese a handful of freshly grated

Preheat the oven to 220°C/425°F/Gas Mark 7. Season the beef with salt and pepper, then wrap the streaky bacon slices around the fillet, secure with string and sprinkle with oil.

Place the meat on a trivet in a roasting tray and pour about 1 glass of water into the tray. Place the garlic heads cut-side up next to the beef and drizzle the cut surfaces with oil. Cook in the oven for about 20 minutes, then remove the bacon and cook for a further 10 minutes. Remove from the oven and leave aside to rest.

To make the spicy butter, place the roasted pepper and chilli and the anchovies in a food processor and whiz to a purée. Add the butter, chilli powder and Parmesan to the purée and whiz again until everything is well blended. Scrape out onto clingfilm or foil and shape into a roll. Secure with the clingfilm or foil and put in the fridge or freezer to set (if using a freezer, remove about 15 minutes before use).

To serve, carve the beef into thick slices and top with slices of the chilli butter, which will melt on to and into the beef. Garnish with the heads of softly roasted garlic and chopped parsley.

loin of pork
with prunes

Make sure that the skin of the loin of pork is finely scored and don't forget to dry the skin and then rub in some salt, as this way you will have a lovely crackling.

Loin of pork 1.75 kg/4 lb, boned and rind removed

Potatoes 900 g/2 lb, peeled and cut into large pieces

Onion 1, peeled and cut into chunks

Fresh rosemary sprigs of

For the stuffing

Dried, stoned prunes 225 g/8 oz

Armagnac a hefty splash of

Orange juice 2 tablespoons

Good olive oil 150 ml/5 fl oz

Fresh parsley a handful of chopped

Fresh chives 1 tablespoon chopped

Rosemary sprigs a handful of fresh

Salt and pepper

Serves 6–8

To make the stuffing, tip the prunes into a bowl, cover with the Armagnac and orange juice and leave for at least 6 hours to soak and reconstitute.

When the prunes have soaked up all the booze, place them in a food processor with a good splash of the oil, the parsley, chives, most of the rosemary and salt and pepper to taste and pulse briefly to chop roughly (not purée).

Preheat the oven to 200°C/400°F/Gas Mark 6. Place the pork loin on a board, fat-side up, and, using a sharp knife, cut it down the middle (but not right through to the board) and open up the sides to create a flat surface for stuffing. Spread over the prune stuffing, close the loin back up again and secure with string. Dust the skin with salt.

Parboil the potatoes for about 5 minutes, then drain and chuck in a roasting tray with the onion and the remaining oil and rosemary. Roast in the oven for about 30 minutes, then place a rack on top of the vegetables in the tray and place the pork loin fat-side up in the rack and roast for another hour or so until the pork is tender. Serve with the potatoes and onions.

roast leg of lamb

Small legs of milk-fed lamb are far and away the best. Unfashionable for some, but essential for me, the lamb should be served pink.

To enjoy a really good roast **leg of lamb**, you must first go shopping. Buy a good leg, buy a tin of **anchovies** in olive oil, two or three heads of **garlic**, 1 **carrot**, 1 big **onion**, a branch of **rosemary**, some **spuds**, some **double cream** and some **dry white wine**.

When you get back to the kitchen, peel all the garlic and finely slice a few cloves, then peel the carrot and onion and chop them into very small pieces. Peel some spuds and slice them very, very thinly, then rinse them in water to remove the starch and dry them. Look around the kitchen for a nice earthenware dish for the potato part and a good-sized, deep, roasting tray with a trivet for the roasting part.

Make sure the oven is set at about 200°C/400°F/Gas Mark 6 (180°C if you have a fan oven, but if you have the choice don't use the fan setting). Make incisions all over the lamb leg and slide in anchovy fillets and slivers of garlic, studded so that it is like a medieval knight's breastplate.

Put the chopped onion and carrot underneath the trivet, then place the studded lamb upon the trivet and splash in about half the bottle of white wine. Rub the lamb with some **olive oil** (which I assume you already have in your kitchen), put the rosemary on top and pop in quite high up in the oven. Don't be scared, don't be tempted to cover the lamb, and don't reduce the temperature. If halfway through the cooking, the liquid underneath is reducing, add a little more wine or some water, because this is where your gravy will come from.

Meanwhile, crush some more garlic very finely, rub it around your earthenware dish and layer in the very finely sliced potatoes. Season well with salt and pepper, cover with double cream, cover the dish with cooking foil and put in the lower half of the oven.

After about 1½ hours, take out the leg of lamb and put on a warm dish, cover with foil and leave to rest in a warm place for at least 40 minutes. Remove the foil from the potatoes and swap to the upper shelf in the oven to allow them to go golden.

Strain the juices from the lamb roasting tray into a pan, and reduce until you have a fine lamb, wine and vegetable-flavoured sauce. Serve the lamb with the potatoes and sauce.

It is just as simple as that.

roast shoulder
of lamb

Now the shoulder is a different story. With lots of lovely fat, it can take slower, longer cooking and stay moist. Forget the cholesterol problems, it is full of flavour.

Get a good **shoulder of lamb**, some **spuds**, **onions**, **garlic** and some **chicken or vegetable stock** from the supermarket (which, by the way, is perfectly acceptable these days).

Firstly, peel the potatoes and slice very thinly, then rinse and pat dry. Peel about half the onions and slice very, very finely. Peel and crush some garlic and make a layer cake of onions, garlic and potatoes in the bottom of your roasting tray. Whack in a bit of **salt** and **pepper**, a dash of **olive oil** and maybe a **sprig of rosemary** on top and pour in a little stock.

Place the lamb on a rack in the oven and place the tray of potatoes, onions and garlic directly underneath, so that the roasting juices from the lamb will drop into the potatoes.

After about 1½ hours, take out the lamb and put on a warm dish, cover with cooking foil and leave to rest in a warm place for at least 40 minutes.

Pour any juices that have come from the lamb into the potato dish and transfer it to a higher shelf in the oven. Cook until it is nicely browned, a bit like a good old-fashioned Lancashire hot pot. Serve with the lamb.

in a stew

There is nothing more satisfying on a cold day than a steaming casserole or plate of stew. And if you plan your shopping and cooking carefully, there is no need to get your culinary knickers in a twist. You can always prepare your stew well in advance and if you make too much you can freeze the residue. Give yourself plenty of time, use good, heavy cast-iron pots with lids and cook gently and slowly.

cockerel in red wine

This is where you have to make friends and influence a stallholder at your local farmers' market. If you can't get a cockerel, get the oldest boiler you can find. Always use the best-quality wine you can afford.

Unsalted butter and olive oil for frying

Button mushrooms 200 g/7 oz, sliced

Bacon 200 g/7 oz, finely diced

Button onions or shallots 200 g/7 oz, peeled but left whole

Cockerel or boiler 1 whole, about 2 kg/4½ lb, cut into joints

Seasoned plain flour 2 tablespoons

Glass brandy 1 small

Good red wine (such as a Burgundy) 1 bottle

Onion 1 large, peeled and roughly chopped

Carrot 1, peeled and cut into large pieces

Garlic 3 cloves, peeled and crushed

Bouquet garni 1 (fresh thyme, parsley stalks and 1 bay leaf, tied together with string)

Chicken livers 2, minced (optional)

Salt and pepper

Serves 6

Heat a large knob of butter and a good splash of oil in a large ovenproof casserole with a lid and fry the mushrooms, bacon and button onions or shallots until brown. Remove from the pan and set aside.

Using the same pan, brown the chicken joints on both sides, season with salt and pepper and sprinkle over the flour.

Pour the brandy over the chicken and set alight. When the flames subside, pour over the wine, add the chopped onion, carrot, garlic and bouquet garni and bring up to the boil.

Lower the heat, cover the pan and simmer gently over a low heat for 1 hour.

Return the mushrooms, bacon and button onions or shallots to the pan and cook for a further 1 hour.

When the chicken is cooked and tender, remove and discard the bouquet garni, add the minced chicken livers (if using) and cook for a further 5 minutes.

Check for seasoning and serve.

flamed pheasant
with cider and
calvados

Why not try this magnificent recipe for Christmas Day or New Year's Day and kick the turkey into touch! You must allow half a pheasant per person.

Unsalted butter 50 g/2 oz

Olive oil for frying

Oven-ready pheasants 2 large, each cut into 4 portions

Seasoned plain flour about 2½ tablespoons

Calvados 1 small glass

Bacon 4 rashers of, cut into lardons

Onions 2, peeled and finely chopped

Celery sticks 2, stringed and finely chopped

Crisp eating apples 4, core removed, cut into quarters

Fresh root ginger 2.5 cm/1 inch piece of, peeled and grated

Juniper berries 1 tablespoon, crushed

Chicken stock 300 ml/10 fl oz

Dry cider 750 ml/1¼ pints

Lemon juice 1 tablespoon

Double cream 150 ml/5 fl oz

Salt and pepper

Serves 6

Preheat the oven to 170°C/340°F/Gas Mark 3.

Heat the butter with a little oil in a heavy-based ovenproof casserole with a lid. Dust the pheasants with about half the seasoned flour and fry until golden on both sides.

Pour over the Calvados and set alight. When the flames have subsided, remove the pheasant from the pan and set aside.

Using the same pan, add the bacon and fry for a couple of minutes, then add the onions, celery, apples, ginger and juniper (add a little more oil if necessary).

Sprinkle over another spoonful of flour and stir well, then add the stock, cider and lemon juice, season with salt and pepper and bring to the boil, stirring all the time.

Lower the heat to a simmer and add the pheasant pieces, then cover the pan and cook in the oven for about 1 hour.

When the pheasant is tender, remove from the casserole and set aside to keep warm. Strain the sauce through a sieve, discard the vegetables etc., and return the sauce to the casserole dish.

Add the cream and bring back to the boil on the hob, then reduce the heat and simmer for about 10 minutes.

Return the pheasant to the casserole dish, check for seasoning and serve.

beef simmered
in guinness
or stout

Simmered gently, this is a rich, rewarding and heartwarming stew. By the way, it is even better the next day.

Stewing beef, such as chuck, blade or skirt 1.25 kg/2½ lb, cut into large chunks

Plain flour 2 tablespoons seasoned

Olive oil for frying

Red onions 2 large, peeled and sliced

Carrots 450 g/1 lb, peeled and cut into rounds

Tomato purée 1 tablespoon

Guinness or stout 450 ml/15 fl oz

Water 450 ml/15 fl oz

Bay leaves 2

Brown sugar 2 teaspoons

Cider vinegar 1 teaspoon

Salt and pepper

Serves 6

Preheat the oven to 150°C/300°F/Gas Mark 2. Roll the steak in half the seasoned flour until thoroughly coated.

Heat a good splash of oil in a large flameproof casserole with a lid and fry the beef, a few pieces at a time, until browned on all sides. Lift each batch out of the pan and set aside while you cook the rest.

When all the meat is browned, add the onions to the pan and cook until they are lightly browned, then add the carrots, stirring well to coat them with the cooking juices.

Sprinkle in the remaining flour, add the tomato purée and put the meat back into the pan, along with any juices that are on the plate. Pour over the Guinness or stout and water and stir, then add the bay leaves and sugar.

Cover the pan and cook in the oven for 1½ hours.

Add the vinegar and cook for 30 minutes. Serve immediately, or, even better, reheat the next day.

beef stew with lots of carrots

This is one of my wife's great specialities and when all my boozy rugby friends come round she produces a vat of it. It is always served with mashed potato and the old red wine splashes down a treat as you cheer on your losing team!

Stewing beef, such as blade, chuck or shin 900 g/2 lb, cut into nice big chunks

Seasoned flour 2 tablespoons for dusting

Red onions 2, peeled and cut into thick slices

Carrots 750 g/1½ lb, peeled and cut into large chunks

Head of celery 1, stringed and cut into large chunks

Mixed herbs 1 teaspoon dried

Chopped tomatoes 400 g/13 oz can

Tomato purée 1 tablespoon

Worcestershire sauce 1 tablespoon

Good beef stock 1 litre/1¾ pints

Water 500 ml/17 fl oz

Bay leaves 3

Anchovy essence a good splash of bottled

Unsalted butter and olive oil for frying

Salt and pepper

Serves 6

Preheat the oven to 150°C/300°F/Gas Mark 2. Dust the beef chunks in plenty of seasoned flour until well coated.

Heat a large knob of butter and a good splash of oil in a heavy-based, flameproof casserole with a lid and fry the beef, a few pieces at a time, until browned on all sides. Lift each batch out of the pan and set aside while you cook the rest.

Using the same pan, fry the onions until they are browned and softening.

Add the carrots and celery and stir well to coat in the butter, oil and cooking juices. Sprinkle on the dried herbs and stir well, then add the tomatoes, tomato purée, Worcestershire sauce and a very good grind of black pepper and mix well.

Return the meat to the pan, along with any juices that are on the plate, mix well and pour over the stock and water. Throw in the bay leaves and a good shake of anchovy essence and bring to the boil. Lower the heat to a simmer, cover the pan and cook in the oven for about 3 hours until the meat is tender.

Check for seasoning and serve.

burgundy beef in red wine

Use chunks of grainy shin of beef or flank; avoid fatless cuts like topside. This is a slow-cooked dish and the fat melts into the sauce.

Butter and olive oil for frying

Stewing beef, such as shin, chuck, blade, flank or silverside 1.5 kg/3½ lb, cut into 3.5–5cm/1½–2 inch cubes

Bacon 100 g/3½ oz diced

Onions 2, peeled and finely chopped

Carrots 2, peeled and finely chopped

Plain flour 2 tablespoons

Burgundy red wine 1½ bottles

Garlic 2 cloves, peeled and finely chopped

Bouquet garni 1

Salt and pepper

Serves 6

Heat a big knob of butter with a good splash of oil in a large ovenproof casserole and fry the beef and bacon until brown all over.

Add the onions and carrots and cook until they are just softening and changing colour, then sprinkle over the flour and stir well to soak up the juices. Pour in the wine so that all the ingredients are covered, add the garlic and bouquet garni, season with salt and pepper and bring to the boil. Lower the heat, cover the pan and cook for 2–3 hours.

When the meat is tender, remove from the pan. Discard the bouquet garni. Simmer the sauce for another 10 minutes or so to slightly reduce and thicken it. Check for seasoning.

Return the meat to the pan to reheat and then serve.

pork casserole with apricots

A good old-fashioned dish with a nice mix of savoury and sweet flavours. Cider is the ideal alcohol to use in this dish as it has such an affinity with pork.

Vegetable oil for frying

Shallots 8, peeled but kept whole

Mushrooms 125 g/4 oz, quartered

Pork fillet 450 g/1 lb, thickly sliced

Seasoned flour 1 large tablespoon, for dusting

Garlic 1 clove, peeled and finely chopped

Vegetable stock 300 ml/10 fl oz

Dry cider 150 ml/5 fl oz

Tomato purée 1 tablespoon

Dried apricots 75 g/3 oz

Dried, mixed herbs a good pinch of

Salt and pepper

Preheat the oven to 170°C/340°F/Gas Mark 3.

Heat a good splash of oil in a large heavy-based flameproof casserole with a lid and fry the shallots and mushrooms until softened and browned.

Roll the pork fillet in the seasoned flour and add to the shallots and mushrooms. Add the garlic and stir. Lower the heat, add the stock, cider and tomato purée and stir well.

Add the apricots and mixed herbs and season with salt and pepper, then stir and bring to a simmer.

Cover the casserole and cook in the oven for 1–1½ hours until tender.

rabbit casserole
with sherry
and red wine

Rabbit is highly underrated nowadays, but has a delicate, white flesh with more flavour than chicken. However, the red wine in this recipe will make this a dark, rich dish. Make friends with your local gamekeeper (or poacher) and get a freshly killed wild rabbit.

Rabbit joints 1.4 kg/3 lb

Seasoned plain flour 2 tablespoons

Unsalted butter and olive oil for frying

Streaky bacon 3 rashers of, cut into lardons

Onions 2 large, peeled and finely chopped

Carrots 350 g/12 oz, peeled and finely chopped

Celery sticks 2, stringed and finely chopped

Fennel 2 bulbs of, sliced

Dry sherry 150 ml/5 fl oz

Chicken stock 600 ml/1 pint

Redcurrant jelly 1 tablespoon

Salt and pepper

For the marinade

Good red wine 600 ml/1 pint

Garlic 4 cloves, peeled and finely chopped

Bay leaves 2

Thyme leaves fresh

Serves 6

To make the marinade, pour the wine into a large dish and stir in the garlic, bay leaves and thyme. Drop in the rabbit joints and place in the fridge to marinate for several hours. Every so often, turn the rabbit joints to ensure they are well covered on all sides.

When ready to cook, preheat the oven to 170°C/340°F/Gas Mark 3. Remove the rabbit from the marinade and reserve the marinade. Pat the rabbit dry with kitchen paper and roll it in a little of the flour.

Heat a large knob of butter and a good splash of oil in a large heavy-based casserole with a lid. Fry the rabbit joints on both sides until golden, then remove from the pan and set aside.

Using the same pan, add the bacon and fry for a couple of minutes, then add the onions and fry for a couple of minutes. Add all the other vegetables and cook over a low heat for about 10 minutes. Stir in the remaining flour and cook for a couple of minutes.

Return the rabbit joints to the pan, pour in the sherry, stock and reserved marinade and bring to a simmer. Cover the pan and cook in the oven for about 1½ hours.

When the rabbit is tender, place the joints on a warm serving dish, cover with cooking foil and keep warm in a very low oven.

Strain the sauce and return to the casserole. Add the redcurrant jelly and simmer on the hob for 10 minutes until thickened. Season with salt and pepper.

Pour the sauce over the rabbit and serve.

simmered lamb
with spring
vegetables

The tenderest of young lamb, the freshest of little spring vegetables. It is important to use a Cos lettuce since a tender-leafed lettuce will disintegrate and lose its texture and flavour. This is a super dish for Easter.

Leg of spring lamb 1, about 1.75 kg/4 lb

Unsalted butter 175 g/6 oz

Baby leeks 450 g/1 lb, cut into 3.5 cm/1½ inch batons

Cos lettuce ½ dark green, ripped into rough pieces

Fresh parsley 1 bunch of, finely chopped

Salt and pepper

For the sauce

Egg yolks 4

Eggs 2

Unsalted butter 1 large tablespoon

Plain flour 1 tablespoon

Lemons juice of 5 or 6

Serves 6

Cut the lamb off the bone into bite-sized pieces (you could ask your butcher to do this for you).

Melt half the butter in a large heavy-based casserole with a lid and fry the lamb, a few pieces at a time, until browned on all sides. Lift each batch out of the pan and set aside while you cook the rest – do not over-fry as spring lamb is very tender. Return all the lamb to the pan.

Stir in the leeks and soften for a few minutes, then add the torn lettuce, the remaining butter and a couple of cups of water. Season with salt and pepper and stir well, then cover the pan, lower the heat and simmer very gently for 40–45 minutes.

When you think the lamb is almost cooked, strain off a cupful or so of the cooking liquid, leaving a small amount in the pan. Stir the parsley into the lamb.

To make the sauce, beat the egg yolks together with the eggs. Melt the butter in a pan, add the flour and whisk well to make a smooth roux (paste). Slowly whisk in the cooking liquid from the pan until smooth, then lower the heat and whisk in the lemon juice until you have the consistency of double cream. Remove the pan from the heat and slowly add the beaten eggs to the sauce, whisking rapidly to avoid lumps or curdling. This will thicken the sauce.

Place the lamb and vegetables on a hot serving dish, pour over the lemon sauce and serve immediately.

lamb and chickpea casserole

Apart from butterbeans, chickpeas are one of my favourite pulses and they go beautifully with lamb. The heady smell of cumin and the golden glow of the turmeric give this dish a very North African feel.

Lamb 1 kg/2¼ lb, cut into bite-sized pieces

Ground sweet paprika 1 teaspoon

Ground cumin 1 teaspoon

Clarified butter 50 g/2 oz

Onions 2 large, peeled and sliced

Ground turmeric ½ teaspoon

Chopped tomatoes 2 x 400 g/13 oz cans

Caster sugar 2 teaspoons

Chickpeas 300 g/11 oz can

Fresh thyme 2 teaspoons chopped

Salt and pepper

Fresh parsley a handful of chopped, to garnish

Serves 6

Mix the lamb, paprika and cumin in a large bowl, cover and leave overnight in the fridge.

Heat the butter in a heavy-based pan. Add the lamb and spice mixture and the onions and stir all this together until the onions start to soften.

Stir in the turmeric, then add the tomatoes and sugar, cover the pan and simmer for about 40 minutes, or until the lamb is tender.

Add the chickpeas and thyme and simmer, uncovered, for another 10–15 minutes.

Season to taste, garnish with chopped parsley and serve.

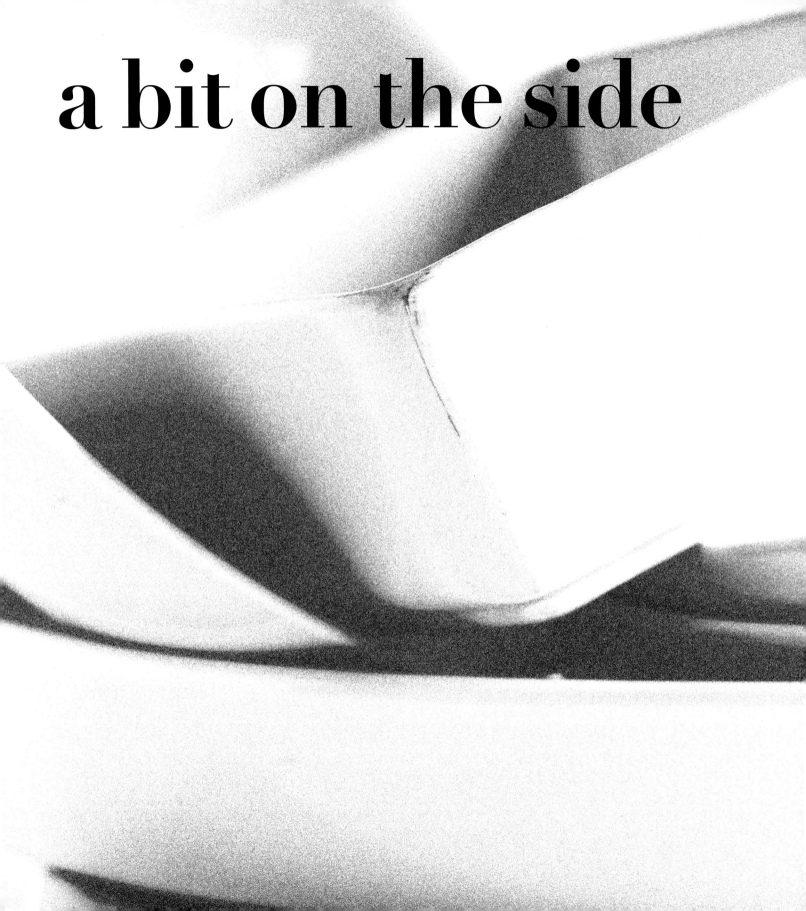

a bit on the side

One of the great things nowadays is the huge variety of vegetables and leaves that are available to us in the supermarkets and at farmers' markets. The selection available has made cooking with vegetables and creating salads much more exciting than it was in previous days. Of course, the wonderful staples that this country provides from season to season are fantastic. Root vegetables, great runner beans, lettuces, peas, tomatoes, and so on, still make the most marvellous accompaniments to other dishes and should never be dismissed.

In addition to the obvious benefits of vegetables and salads, as far as fibre and vitamins go, it is now possible to create superb main meals using herbs, spices and imagination. I do not believe in the word vegetarian, I believe in cooking with vegetables.

new potatoes with mushrooms and glazed onions

Sweet little onions and nutty potatoes, lightly scrubbed, is a dish on its own. I love rosemary with potatoes, but do not add too much as it can taste soapy.

New potatoes, such as Jersey Royals 900 g/2 lb scrubbed

Unsalted butter and olive oil for frying

Wild mushrooms, such as girolles, morels, etc. 750 g/1½ lb, or you could use chestnut mushrooms

Shallot 1, peeled and finely chopped

Fresh thyme 1 sprig of

Fresh rosemary leaves a few, finely chopped

Baby onions or shallots 225 g/8 oz, peeled but left whole

Caster sugar 1 tablespoon

Salt and pepper

Serves 6

Parboil the potatoes for 5 minutes or so, then drain well.

Heat a good splash of oil in a heavy-based sauté pan and sauté the potatoes until they are cooked through and golden brown. Set aside and keep warm.

Heat a knob of butter in another pan and sauté the mushrooms with the chopped shallot, thyme, rosemary and salt and pepper to taste, until the shallot is softened and translucent. Set aside and keep warm.

Place the baby onions or shallots in another pan, just cover them with water and add a knob of butter and the sugar. Bring to the boil, then reduce the heat and simmer, uncovered, for about 15 minutes, or until the onions are cooked and the water has evaporated. The onions should be lightly browned and glazed.

Combine all the ingredients in a serving dish, mix well and serve.

baked aubergines

Aubergines are a lovely exotic vegetable, redolent of the sunshine of the Mediterranean. I cook this dish a lot when I am in France and it can be served hot or cold.

Olive oil for frying

Aubergines 3 large, cut in slices and salted in a colander for 1 hour, then rinsed and dried

Garlic 2 cloves, peeled and crushed

Passata (liquid tomatoes) 400 ml/14 fl oz

Cheese of your choice, such as Parmesan or Cheddar or similar 100 g/3½ oz grated

Fine breadcrumbs 40 g/1½ oz

Butter a large knob of

Flour for dusting

Salt and pepper

Serves 4–6

Preheat the oven to 180°/350°F/Gas Mark 4. Coat the aubergine slices in flour.

Heat a large slug of oil in a pan and fry the aubergines, turning once, until brown on both sides.

Stir the garlic into the passata.

Oil a casserole dish and arrange a layer of half the fried aubergines on the bottom. Pour on half of the passata and then sprinkle some cheese on top. Layer on the remaining aubergine slices, passata and cheese. Top with the breadcrumbs and dot butter over the top to help crisp and brown the dish.

Cook in the oven for about 20 minutes until hot and bubbling, and brown on top.

okra with onion and tomato

Okra are known as ladies fingers. They are long and thin and worthy of kissing. However, halfway through cooking the okra can appear sticky and beyond help, but this will right itself.

Olive oil for frying

Baby onions or shallots 12, peeled and cut in half

Okra 750 g/1½ lb, tops removed

Garlic 2 cloves, peeled and crushed

Ground cumin 2 teaspoons

Ground cinnamon 1 teaspoon

Ground allspice ½ teaspoon

Chopped tomatoes 400 g/13 oz can

Chicken stock 300 ml/10 fl oz

Salt and pepper

Fresh parsley chopped, to garnish

Serves 6

Heat a large splash of oil in a pan, add the onions or shallots and fry, stirring occasionally, for about 15 minutes until the onions are brown. Remove from the pan and set aside.

Heat a little more oil in the same pan, add the okra, garlic and spices and cook gently for 5–7 minutes until the okra is slightly coloured and the spices are fragrant.

Tip the onions into the pan with the tomatoes and stock, season with salt and pepper and simmer, uncovered, for 35–40 minutes, stirring occasionally, until the sauce has thickened and the vegetables are soft.

Garnish with chopped parsley and serve.

carrot and
sweet potato
with honey

Bored with jacket potatoes? Try this sweet, colourful alternative.

Carrots 4 medium, peeled and cut into chunks

Sweet potatoes 2, peeled and cut into chunks

Unsalted butter 50 g/2 oz, melted

Olive oil a good slug of

Ground cumin 1½ teaspoons

Cumin seeds 1 teaspoon

Honey 1 tablespoon

Fresh parsley a handful of chopped, to garnish

Preheat the oven to 200°C/400°F/Gas Mark 6.

Boil some water in a pan, add the carrots and sweet potatoes and cook for 5 minutes, then drain.

In a bowl, mix the butter with the oil, ground cumin, cumin seeds and honey.

Place the carrots and sweet potatoes on a wire rack over a baking tray and brush well with the sweet butter mixture. Cook in the oven for 20–25 minutes, basting regularly with the butter mixture.

Serve garnished with chopped parsley.

roasted stuffed mixed peppers

Roasted red and yellow peppers, properly prepared, will glow like the sun rising over the Indian Ocean. Using green peppers as well just varies the look. They taste the same.

mixed peppers 4, halved, seeds and pith removed

vegetable oil for frying

For the masala flavouring

Cumin seeds 1 teaspoon

Minced garlic 1 teaspoon

Grated ginger 1 teaspoon

Garam masala ½ teaspoon (you can buy this)

Red chilli powder ½ teaspoon

For the stuffing

Mixed vegetables, such as carrots, white cabbage, onion, peas, green beans a selection of, very finely chopped

Raisins or sultanas 1 tablespoon

Cashew nuts 1 tablespoon chopped

Feta cheese or similar 1 cup of, cut into very fine cubes

Fresh coriander leaves a good handful of, chopped

Preheat the oven to 200°C/400°F/Gas Mark 6.

For the masala flavouring, heat a good splash of oil in a pan, throw in the cumin seeds, shake the pan and cook until they 'crackle'. Stir in the rest of the masala ingredients and cook for 20 or so seconds until they release their aromas.

Add the stuffing vegetables and stir-fry until they are well mixed with the masala and slightly softened. Remove from the heat and set aside to cool.

Once the mixture has cooled, add the raisins or sultanas, the nuts, cheese and chopped coriander.

Fill the peppers with this mixture. Brush the peppers with oil, place in a baking tray or dish and bake in the oven until the peppers have softened, about 15–20 minutes.

Serve at once

artichokes braised in wine

When fully grown, an artichoke flowers like a magnificent thistle, but you will need to use small, tender artichokes for this recipe.

Artichokes 6 small, stalks and tough outer leaves removed

Lemon juice of ½

Olive oil a good slug of

Onion 1, peeled and finely chopped

Garlic 2 cloves, peeled and finely sliced

Dry white wine 225 ml/8 fl oz

Salt

Nutmeg freshly grated, to serve

Serves 6

Cut the artichokes into quarters and remove the hairy choke. Immediately drop the artichokes into a large bowl of water with the lemon juice. This will stop them discolouring. When you have prepared all the artichokes, drain them and pat them dry with kitchen paper.

Heat the oil in a large pan and sauté the onion and garlic gently for 5 minutes or so.

Add the artichokes and toss around in the oil for a bit until well coated with all the flavours.

Pour in the wine, a sprinkling of salt and enough water to cover the artichokes. Bring to the boil, then lower the heat, cover the pan and simmer for about 10 minutes.

Remove the lid and simmer for another 30 minutes.

Drain and serve with a sprinkling of fresh nutmeg.

chickpeas with lime and chilli

This is a wonderful zingy, tangy dish. Do not be tempted to substitute lemons for limes in this dish, they simply do not have the same unique flavour.

Olive oil for frying

Red onion 1 large, peeled and finely sliced

Ground cumin 1 teaspoon

Ground coriander 1 teaspoon

Red chilli 1 large, deseeded and finely chopped

Chickpeas 400 g/13 oz can, drained and rinsed

Chicken stock 300 ml/10 fl oz

Chopped tomatoes 400 g/13 oz can

Caster sugar a pinch of

Limes juice and zest of 3

Salt and pepper

Fresh coriander leaves a big handful of chopped, to garnish

Heat a glug of oil in a large pan and gently fry the onion with the ground cumin and coriander and chopped chilli until the onion is just turning soft.

Add the chickpeas, stock, tomatoes, sugar and salt and pepper to taste, lower the heat and simmer for about 20 minutes.

Add the lime juice and zest and continue to cook for another 5 minutes, then spoon into a serving dish and sprinkle with the chopped coriander.

green beans with tomato and walnuts

The walnuts add a nice crunch to this dish (don't forget to skin them first though). This dish is best served cold as a salad.

Olive oil for frying

Green beans 1 kg/2¼ lb, topped and tailed

Garlic 2 cloves, peeled and crushed

Ground coriander 2 teaspoons

Cayenne pepper ¼ teaspoon

Chopped walnuts 100 g/3½ oz, toasted in a dry frying pan

Passata 400 g/13 oz can

Caster sugar 1 teaspoon

Fresh coriander leaves a large handful of

Red pepper 1, deseeded and pith removed, thinly sliced

Yellow pepper 1, deseeded and pith removed, thinly sliced

Salt and pepper

Serves 6

Boil the beans in salted water until tender, then drain and set aside.

Heat a glug of oil in another pan, add the garlic, spices and nuts and cook until fragrant.

Add the passata, sugar and coriander leaves and heat through.

Remove from the heat and add the beans and peppers, then mix all the ingredients well.

battered, deep-fried vegetables

Be sure to cut the vegetables into very thin slices, cover them liberally with salt and place on kitchen paper so the liquid escapes before they are fried in vegetable oil. Rinse and dry them before frying. These need to be enjoyed hot and straight out of the pan.

A good selection of vegetables, such as potatoes, aubergines, courgettes, peppers, mushrooms, onions, peeled, washed, cut to size as desired and salted (see above)

Vegetable oil for frying

For the batter

Chickpea flour 2 cups of

Chilli powder 1 teaspoon

Salt 1 teaspoon

Bicarbonate of soda ½ teaspoon

Mix all the ingredients for the batter in a bowl, then add enough water to make a smooth batter with the consistency of double cream. Cover and place in the fridge to rest for about 30 minutes.

Heat enough oil for deep-frying (about 5 cm/2 inches) in a deep pan. Dip the vegetables into the batter, drop into the hot oil in batches and cook until they float to the surface and are crisp and golden.

Drain on kitchen paper and serve.

braised onions

Do try to buy the very tiny, red-skinned onions for this recipe as they are sweeter. If not, substitute shallots.

Onions 500 g/1 lb 2 oz very small, peeled and left whole

Garlic 3 cloves, peeled

Olive oil a good slug of

Peppercorns 6

Clove 1

Paprika ½ teaspoon

White wine 50 ml/2 fl oz

Bay leaf 1

Salt

Serves 6

Put the onions, garlic, oil, peppercorns and clove into a large saucepan over a medium heat and toss to coat in the oil. Do not let the onions brown.

Add the paprika, wine, bay leaf and salt to taste, cover the pan and cook slowly until the onions are tender, shaking the pan every so often to prevent burning, about 25 minutes in all.

mushrooms with sherry

The joy of this dish is that you can gather mushrooms from the fields or the forest (do be careful) or you can buy little button ones from the supermarket. Always buy button mushrooms that are tightly closed with no gills showing. Alternatively, use chestnut mushrooms, they have more flavour.

Olive oil for frying

Mushrooms, such as flat field mushrooms or chestnut mushrooms 500 g/1 lb 2 oz, sliced

Onion ½, peeled and finely chopped

Garlic 2 cloves, peeled and finely chopped

Dry sherry 125 ml/4 fl oz

Salt and pepper

To garnish

Egg 1 hard-boiled, chopped

Fresh parsley chopped

Heat a glug of oil in a frying pan and sauté the mushrooms until they stop releasing their liquid.

Add the onion and garlic and cook until browned.

Add the sherry, season with salt and pepper and simmer for about 10 minutes.

Transfer to a serving dish and garnish with chopped egg and parsley.

valencia-style peas

Peas are one of the most versatile vegetables in the cook's repertoire. Here is a nice spicy version that will go perfectly with lamb cutlets or pork.

Olive oil for frying

Garlic 2 cloves, peeled

Onion 1, peeled and chopped

Frozen peas 1 kg/2¼ lb

Pernod 1 tablespoon

White wine 100 ml/3½ fl oz

Bay leaf 1

Fresh thyme 2 sprigs of

Saffron ¼ teaspoon

Ground cumin ¼ teaspoon

Salt and pepper

To garnish

Red pepper 1, deseeded and pith removed, cut into fine strips

Fresh parsley a good handful of chopped

Serves 8

Heat a glug of oil in a large pan. Finely chop 1 garlic clove, add to the pan with the onion and sauté for about 3 minutes, but do not let the garlic burn.

Add the peas and stir well, then add the Pernod, wine, bay leaf and thyme. Simmer gently, uncovered, for about 5 minutes.

Crush the other garlic clove in a mortar and pestle with the saffron and ground cumin. Add a little water to the mix and then add it to the peas. Season with salt and pepper and simmer for a further 5 minutes.

Garnish with the red pepper strips and chopped parsley.

pease pudding

When I was a cold and hungry kid, my mother would produce this huge tray of pease pudding. Never salt pulses before cooking as this can make them tough; season at the end.

Split yellow peas 225 g/8 oz, placed in a bowl, covered with cold water and soaked overnight

Fresh thyme 2 teaspoons chopped

Fresh mint 2 teaspoons chopped

Carrot 1, peeled

Onion 1, peeled

Celery stick 1, stringed

Smoked bacon a piece of

Bay leaf 1

Egg yolk 1

Butter a generous knob of

Salt and pepper

Cut a large square of muslin cloth. Drain the peas and tip onto the cloth. Sprinkle with the herbs, pull the edges of the muslin together and secure tightly with string.

Pour some water into a large pan, add the carrot, onion, celery, bacon and bay leaf and bring to the boil. Lower the heat, add the split pea bag, cover the pan and simmer for about 3 hours.

Remove the bag from the stock and allow to cool, then turn the pease pudding out into a bowl.

Mash well, then add the egg yolk and the butter and beat well until light and fluffy. Season well with salt and pepper.

Serve with the meat of your choice.

fresh broad beans sautéed with smoked ham

First, chill your rosé wine; second, get your partner (a word I hate) to prepare the beans. Unless you grow your own beans, it is almost impossible to get them young and tender. However, if you can find young ones, you do not need to peel them. This should serve about 4–6 people alongside a main course.

Pod and peel 2 kg/4½ lb of **broad beans**. Blanch in lightly salted, boiling water and drain.

Cut some **smoked ham** or **bacon** into very small cubes and sauté in a dash of **olive oil**. Add a little crushed **garlic**, stir in the beans and cook until tender.

petit pois, smoked bacon and lettuce

A light, summery recipe and one of my favourite vegetable dishes – the lettuce really lifts it. If you are not a meat eater, don't make this dish as you need the flavour of the bacon in it.

Butter 1 large knob of

Bacon or ham 125 g/4 oz piece of smoked, de-rinded and cut into cubes

White onion 1 medium, peeled and very finely chopped

Petit pois 450 g/1 lb frozen

Crispy lettuce, such as Cos 1 large, coarsely chopped

Chicken stock 600 ml/1 pint

Caster sugar 1 tablespoon

Salt 1 teaspoon

Bay leaf 1

Pepper

Serves 6

Melt the butter in a heavy-based, medium saucepan, and gently fry the cubes of bacon or ham and the onion until the onion is translucent.

Pour in the peas (it doesn't matter if they are still frozen), add the chopped lettuce and cover with the stock. Season with the sugar, salt and a little black pepper and add the bay leaf.

Simmer gently until all the flavours have amalgamated, the lettuce has wilted and the peas are cooked.

spinach with raisins and pine nuts

Add sweetness and crunch to your greens, but remember to cook chard stalks separately and chop the greens.

Raisins or sultanas 50 g/2 oz seedless

Fresh spinach or chard 900 g/2 lb

Garlic 1 clove, peeled and crushed

Pine nuts 3 tablespoons, toasted in a dry frying pan

Olive oil for frying

Salt and pepper

Croûtons, to garnish

Pour some boiling water over the raisins or sultanas and leave them to plump up, then drain.

Pack the spinach or chard into a large saucepan, add a little boiling water and a sprinkling of salt and cook, stirring occasionally, for about 6 minutes.

Drain very well, squeezing out all the excess moisture, then chop the greens.

Heat a good splash of oil in a sauté pan and quickly sauté the garlic for a minute or so.

Add the chopped greens, pine nuts and soaked raisins or sultanas, season with a little salt and pepper and cook for a further 2–3 minutes.

Serve garnished with crunchy croûtons.

pumpkin with saffron

A real sunshine recipe. Beating the mixture with a wooden spoon will add a gloss to this dish. It is a good substitute for mashed potato, but lighter in flavour and texture.

Unsalted butter and olive oil for frying

Pumpkin 350 g/12 oz, peeled, deseeded and cut into chunks

Maize flour 1 tablespoon

Saffron strands a good pinch

Hot milk 1 tablespoon

Milk 50 ml/2 fl oz

Salt and pepper

Heat a big knob of butter and a dash of oil in a heavy-based casserole and very gently sauté the pumpkin – do not let it colour, just become tender.

When soft, mash it with a potato masher.

Dissolve the saffron strands in the hot milk. Stir the flour, saffron infusion and the cold milk into the mashed pumpkin. Beat together well with a wooden spoon, season and return to the heat. Simmer gently for about 5 minutes and serve.

orange, date and almond salad

This is very refreshing and attractive.

Oranges 4 large, peeled and segmented, all pith removed

Dried apricots 50 g/2 oz, halved

Blanched almonds 2 tablespoons, toasted in a dry frying pan

Fresh mint 2 tablespoons chopped

For the dressing

Water 250 ml/8½ fl oz

Star anise 2

Cloves 5

Honey 2 tablespoons

Cinnamon stick 1

Stoned dates 75 g/3 oz, roughly chopped

To make the dressing, mix the water, star anise, cloves, honey and cinnamon in a pan and simmer gently until slightly thickened. Discard the cinnamon stick and star anise, add the dates and cool the mixture.

Mix all the ingredients for the salad in a large bowl and pour over the dressing, mixing well. Serve immediately.

fennel salad

Do try this crunchy salad; it is so delicate, light and flavoursome. Fennel has a wonderful, slightly aniseed flavour and is very refreshing when served raw.

Fennel 3 bulbs

For the dressing
Olive oil a good glug
Lemon juice of ½
Dijon mustard ½ teaspoon
Salt and pepper

Serves 6

Cut the fennel into very fine slices and arrange in a dish.

Whisk together all the ingredients for the dressing and drizzle over the fennel.

green leaf and fresh herb salad

Herbs are not just for decoration, be bold and enjoy them as a salad. However, only use soft herbs and avoid woody ones such as rosemary or thyme.

Watercress 1 bunch of
Rocket leaves 50 g/2 oz
Baby spinach leaves 50 g/2 oz
Fresh flat-leaf parsley 1 large bunch of
Fresh mint leaves 1 bunch of
Fresh coriander leaves 1 bunch of

For the dressing
Olive oil 2 tablespoons
Sunflower oil 2 tablespoons
Lemon juice of 1
Caster sugar a pinch of
Salt and pepper

Put the watercress, rocket and spinach into a large bowl. Tear up the herbs roughly and mix with the leaves.

Whisk together all the ingredients for the dressing and sprinkle over the leaves and herbs, then mix well and serve immediately.

tomato salad with olives and chilli

Tomatoes and chilli go so well together. You can remove the seeds of the chilli for a milder taste.

Tomatoes 4 ripe, cut into quarters

Red onion 1, peeled and sliced

Watercress 1 bunch of

Rocket 1 bunch of

Plump, black olives a large handful of

Fresh red chillies 2 large, cut into fine rings

Fresh coriander leaves 1 tablespoon, roughly chopped

For the dressing

Olive oil 2 tablespoons

Lime juice 1 tablespoon

Caster sugar a pinch of

Fresh rosemary a pinch of chopped

Cumin seeds 1 teaspoon

Garlic 1 clove, peeled and crushed

Whisk together all the ingredients for the dressing.

Assemble the salad ingredients in a large serving dish. Drizzle over the dressing, mix well and serve.

mediterranean mixed salad

This is really a suggestion, use your favourite Mediterranean ingredients.

Ripe tomatoes 4 large, cut into wedges

Red onion 1, peeled, cut in half and finely sliced

Red pepper 1, roasted in the oven until blackened, skin, pith and seeds removed, and cut into strips

Yellow pepper 1, roasted in the oven until blackened, skin, pith and seeds removed, and cut into strips

Fennel 1 bulb of, very finely sliced

Courgette 1, peeled and cut into discs

Fresh basil leaves a large handful

Pitted black olives a good handful

Pine nuts a handful of, toasted in a dry frying pan

Salt and pepper

For the dressing

Olive oil 6 tablespoons

Balsamic vinegar 2 tablespoons

Garlic 1 clove, peeled and crushed

Place the tomatoes, onion, pepper strips, fennel, courgette and basil in a large bowl, season with salt and pepper and toss together.

Whisk together all the ingredients for the dressing and pour over the salad. Sprinkle over the olives and pine nuts and serve immediately.

Index